# Contents

acce [barcode] ory

Hodder & Stoughton

A MEMBER OF THE HODDER HEADLINE GROUP

**Acknowledgements**

The front cover illustration shows a portrait of President Roosevelt, reproduced courtesy of Topham Picture Point.

The publishers would like to thank the following individuals, institutions and companies for permission to reproduce copyright illustrations in this book: © Bettmann/ Corbis, pages 38 and 73; Franklin D. Roosevelt Library, New York/Philadephia Record, *Finis* by Doyle, March 3 1933, page 95.

Every effort has been made to trace and acknowledge ownership of copyright. The publishers will be glad to make suitable arrangements with any copyright holders whom it has not been possible to contact.

Orders: please contact Bookpoint Ltd, 130 Milton Park, Abingdon, Oxon OX14 4SB. Telephone: (44) 01235 827720. Fax: (44) 01235 400454. Lines are open from 9.00-6.00, Monday to Saturday, with a 24 hour message answering service. You can also order through our website www.hodderheadline.co.uk

*British Library Cataloguing in Publication Data*
A catalogue record for this title is available from the British Library

ISBN 0 340 804 297

First published 2001
Impression number   10  9  8  7  6  5  4  3  2
Year                          2007  2006  2005  2004  2003  2002

Typeset by Fakenham Photosetting Limited, Fakenham, Norfolk
Printed in Great  Britain for Hodder & Stoughton Educational,
338 Euston road, London NW1 3BH by The Bath Press, Bath

# Preface

## To the general reader

Although the *Access to History* series has been designed with the needs of students studying the subject at higher examination levels very much in mind, it also has a great deal to offer the general reader. The main body of the text (i.e. ignoring the 'Study Guides' at the ends of chapters) forms a readable and yet stimulating survey of a coherent topic as studied by historians. However, each author's aim has not merely been to provide a clear explanation of what happened in the past (to interest and inform): it has also been assumed that most readers wish to be stimulated into thinking further about the topic and to form opinions of their own about the significance of the events that are described and discussed (to be challenged). Thus, although no prior knowledge of the topic is expected on the reader's part, she or he is treated as an intelligent and thinking person throughout. The author tends to share ideas and possibilities with the reader, rather than passing on numbers of so-called 'historical truths'.

## To the student reader

Although advantage has been taken of the publication of a second edition to ensure the results of recent research are reflected in the text, the main alteration from the first edition is the inclusion of new features, and the modification of existing ones, aimed at assisting you in your study of the topic at AS level, A level and Higher. Two features are designed to assist you during your first reading of a chapter. The *Points to Consider* section following each chapter title is intended to focus your attention on the main theme(s) of the chapter, and the issues box following most section headings alerts you to the question or questions to be dealt with in the section. The *Working on...* section at the end of each chapter suggests ways of gaining maximum benefit from the chapter.

There are many ways in which the series can be used by students studying History at a higher level. It will, therefore, be worthwhile thinking about your own study strategy before you start your work on this book. Obviously, your strategy will vary depending on the aim you have in mind, and the time for study that is available to you.

If, for example, you want to acquire a general overview of the topic in the shortest possible time, the following approach will probably be the most effective:

1. Read chapter 1. As you do so, keep in mind the issues raised in the *Points to Consider* section.
2. Read the *Points to Consider* section at the beginning of chapter 2 and decide whether it is necessary for you to read this chapter.

3. If it is, read the chapter, stopping at each heading or sub-heading to note down the main points that have been made. Often, the best way of doing this is to answer the question(s) posed in the Key Issues boxes.
4. Repeat stage 2 (and stage 3 where appropriate) for all the other chapters.

If, however, your aim is to gain a thorough grasp of the topic, taking however much time is necessary to do so, you may benefit from carrying out the same procedure with each chapter, as follows:

1. Try to read the chapter in one sitting. As you do this, bear in mind any advice given in the *Points to Consider* section.
2. Study the flow diagram at the end of the chapter, ensuring that you understand the general 'shape' of what you have just read.
3. Read the *Working on...* section and decide what further work you need to do on the chapter. In particularly important sections of the book, this is likely to involve reading the chapter a second time and stopping at each heading and sub-heading to think about (and probably to write a summary of) what you have just read.
4. Attempt the *Source-based questions* section. It will sometimes be sufficient to think through your answers, but additional understanding will often be gained by forcing yourself to write them down.

When you have finished the main chapters of the book, study the 'Further Reading' section and decide what additional reading (if any) you will do on the topic.

This book has been designed to help make your studies both enjoyable and successful. If you can think of ways in which this could have been done more effectively, please contact us. In the meantime, we hope that you will gain greatly from your study of History.

*Keith Randell & Robert Pearce*

# 1 A Changing Nation

## POINTS TO CONSIDER

This chapter is intended as an introduction to the study of the USA between the wars. It gives some historical background, an outline of the political system of the USA and examines why the government had grown in the years prior to the 1920s. You should read it as an introduction and background to the interwar period.

## 1 Introduction

In late October 1929, the New York Stock Exchange crashed. Thousands of people lost all the savings they had invested in stocks and shares. Thousands of businesses collapsed. There are stories of businessmen throwing themselves in despair from high ledges of skyscrapers. The Crash was especially shocking because many people believed the economy was doing very well at the time. It was the era of the 'Roaring Twenties', a period of unparalleled prosperity in American history. It was the age of jazz, movies, motor cars and fast living. Now a terrible economic depression set in, with millions out of work, optimism gone, hope forlorn. In 1932, Americans voted Franklin Delano Roosevelt to be their President. He offered new hope with a 'New Deal'. For the first time, the Government would make itself responsible for people's welfare – it would create jobs, offer old age pensions and social security. To many, Roosevelt was a saviour; others saw him as a dictator who increased the role of government to an unacceptable level.

This book covers the interwar period of American history. It will examine the 1920s to see if the decade was really one of fun and optimism, and to consider whether the prosperity was real. It will discuss the causes and effects of the collapse of the stock market and consider the part this played in ushering in the Depression. Life in the depression will be explored and the efforts made to restore prosperity. Finally it will examine in depth the New Deal, what it was and what changes it brought about in the USA.

## 2 Historical Development

> **KEY ISSUE** How did the USA develop as a major power by the 1920s?

The history of the USA is relatively recent. Following their independence from Great Britain in 1783, Americans began to settle their new

The USA

continent with amazing speed. By the mid nineteenth century they had gained all the lands south of Canada and north of Mexico between the Atlantic and Pacific Oceans. This was achieved largely through purchase and warfare. The vast land mass was 3,022,000 square miles in contrast with 94,525 square miles of the United Kingdom. It was settled so quickly that by 1890 the Census declared there was no longer any undeveloped territory available for settlement. Many of the people we shall meet in this book had spent at least the earliest part of their careers in the nineteenth century and still largely held on to its values. The entire history of the USA to 1920 had happened in the space of 140 years. There was little time for the development of tradition as in Europe; the USA was a vast melting pot, where the individual was thought to be of supreme importance and a continent was there to be settled. The fact that it was settled so quickly and the country developed so rapidly led many people to believe in 'the American dream' – that with hard work and initiative one could achieve anything without expecting much help from the government.

It was a land rich in raw materials, fertile for crops and populated by an energetic, dynamic people who were in the main descended from immigrants. The nineteenth century had seen the biggest migration in history, with millions leaving the 'old world' and heading to America where they hoped to find work, land and freedom from persecution.

While the USA may be a single nation, it is also one originally made up of immigrants who had arrived not only from Europe and Asia, but forcibly as slaves from Africa. The Civil War had torn the Union apart in the years 1861 to 1865; it had ended slavery but not the persecution of afro-caribbeans. The North had grown wealthy from industrial development while the South had remained predominantly rural. The West, populated in mythology by pioneers who had, largely by their own efforts, tamed a wilderness, had developed as a region of fierce independence with little toleration of government interference.

The USA had an economic structure in which people were free to make money with very little government interference. Industries grew wealthy partly because of the relative abundance and cheapness of natural resources; partly through the availability of cheap, often immigrant labour; but mainly through the overwhelming demand in a continent advancing so quickly. Huge industrial concerns grew up in the great cities; but small-scale industry also thrived.

## 3 The Political System

| **KEY ISSUE**  How is the USA governed? |
| --- |

The USA has a federal system of government. This means there is both a federal (or central) government situated in Washington DC and also a series of states governments. The USA literally is a union of states, with each cherishing its own rights and customs. There were originally 13 states, but as the continent was settled, others were added. Today there are 50 and in the period covered by this book, 48, with Alaska and Hawaii being subsequently added in 1959. Most states felt they had voluntarily given up some of their own powers to the federal government in Washington. However they jealously guarded those they retained and were wary of any excessive federal government interference.

The USA is a republic, with three arms of federal government.

## a) The Executive

The President heads the executive (or policy-making) branch. He is elected every four years through a complex voting system. Technically speaking, the electorate does not vote directly for the President. There is both a popular vote and electoral college vote in each state. Those who have been chosen to sit in the electoral college cast all their votes for the candidate who has won a majority in the popular vote in that state.

The President is responsible for seeing that the laws are carried out. Traditionally he would ask Congress (the law making body) to draft legislation he favoured. Only very rarely would the President draft laws himself. As we shall see, Roosevelt broke with this tradition during the New Deal years of the 1930s and increasingly produced his own legislation for the approval of Congress. The President has always appointed a Cabinet to help him govern, but the number of presidential staff grew significantly during the New Deal years as the executive took a far more active role in the running of the country. In 1939 the Executive Office of the President was created as a reflection of the huge growth of responsibilities accepted by the executive.

## b) The Legislature

Congress is the legislature in the USA. It has the job of framing the laws. It is divided into two houses:

### i) House of Representatives

This is composed of congressmen directly elected and representing the people of the USA. In particular it has the task of raising revenue.

### ii) Senate

This is composed of 100 senators (during the period covered by this book, 96), two representing each state. The Senate has the power to ratify or reject presidential appointments and may, if necessary, impeach or seek to remove the President or any of his officers.

Both houses need to agree before a law is passed.

## c) The Judiciary

At the head of the judiciary is the Supreme Court. It is made up of nine senior judges (called justices) appointed by the President. Their job is to ensure laws are actually legal and follow the principles of the constitution. Below the Supreme Court there is a network of federal courts spread throughout the country.

The constitution was originally written by the 'Founding Fathers', the men who created the United States in the late eighteenth century. It clearly sets out the different roles of the different branches of government in addition to defining the responsibilities of state governments and outlining individual rights. It was designed to set up a series of 'checks and balances' so no one branch of government could become too powerful. It has been added to over time by amendment, but basically the USA is still governed on the lines set out by the framers of the constitution in the eighteenth century.

However, one thing the framers did not anticipate was the growth of political parties. The main parties in the USA over the course of the twentieth century have been the Republicans and Democrats. In the period covered by this book, the Republicans tended to favour wealth, business and a reduced government role while the Democrats tended to have a wider base of support and adopted a more tolerant line on issues. They tended to find favour increasingly with minority ethnic groups, the less well off and urban dwellers, while the Republicans carried rural areas and small towns, except, as we shall see, in the South where they were seen as the party who freed the slaves after the Civil War. During Roosevelt's period in office there was a significant realignment in political support, with afro-caribbeans in particular turning to his party, the Democrats.

When the majority in either or both houses in Congress is of a different party to the President, he can find it very difficult to govern effectively. He may have to administer laws he disagrees with; often he cannot get Congress to pass laws he wants. The President does have the power to veto or say no to laws he disagrees with, but if both houses agree by a two-thirds majority, they can override his veto.

The Supreme Court too can smother the legislative programme of the administration by declaring laws unconstitutional. This became a huge problem for Roosevelt during the New Deal years. Many felt he was appropriating too much power vis-à-vis the other branches of government and the Supreme Court was to declare much New Deal legislation unconstitutional.

The New Deal overall saw a huge growth in the business of all branches of government and an important issue considered in this book is how far the political system of the USA was changed as a result of it.

# 4 The Growth of Government

> **KEY ISSUE** How did a) Progressivism and b) Involvement in
> World War One lead to the growth of government in the USA?

The New Deal apart, the first decades of the twentieth century saw a considerable growth in the role of federal government. This was due mainly to two developments:

## a) Progressivism

By the turn of the century many Americans were concerned with four major problems. These were corruption in government; social problems such as overcrowding in poor urban areas; social ills such as drunkenness and immorality; and the power of big business to dominate the economy. Large companies called corporations for example often combined together to form 'trusts' which could control the market in their field. They did this by cutting costs of production, setting prices, fixing profits and ensuing others could not compete with them on equal terms. The governments of Presidents T.R. Roosevelt, Taft and Wilson were known as 'Progressive' because they tried to expand their role to address these problems with positive action. In fact, their achievements were relatively disappointing. Despite legislation, they failed in particular to block the power of the giant trusts.

## b) The Entry of the USA into the First World War

The entry of the USA into the war in April 1917 had far reaching effects on the role of federal government. For example 33 percent of the total cost of the war 33 per cent was raised by taxation – in 1918, the highest level of income tax was 77 per cent compared with 7 per cent in 1913. In spring 1918, Congress gave President Wilson almost dictatorial powers over the political and economic life of the nation. Over 500 agencies were set up to control and direct the war effort. In 1918 the Sedition Act made it illegal to criticise the USA, and people who protested about its involvement in the war were sent to prison. After the war was over, many Americans wanted to see the government dismantle these controls, cut taxes and also to stop getting involved in European affairs; this latter policy was known as 'Isolationism'.

**Summary diagram**
The US System of Government

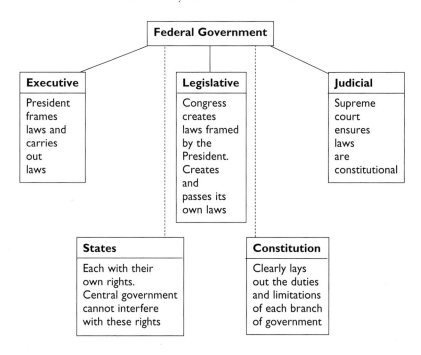

This introductory chapter attempts to introduce the historical development and political system of the USA (sections 1, 2, 3 and 4).

Your notes should be relatively simple and straightforward. There is no need to make notes from section 1, which mainly sets the scene for the whole book.

Your notes on historical development should focus on:

**a)** the speed of settlement and **b)** the differences between North, South and West in the USA.

Your notes on political development should:

**a)** explain what is meant by a federal system of government and constitution, **b)** explain the different roles of the executive, legislature and judiciary, **c)** explain briefly the differences in belief between the Republican and Democratic Parties, and **d)** explain why the President can find it difficult to govern effectively.

Your notes on the Growth of Government should focus on why government grew in the first decades of the twentieth century.

# 2 Problems and Tensions in the 1920s

## POINTS TO CONSIDER

When reading this chapter you need to think about whether Warren Harding's presidency was adequate to address the issues facing the USA in the early 1920s, and how far many of his appointees were simply using office to enrich themselves. You then need to consider the tensions in American society such as the rural–urban divide and the problems caused by prohibition, moral and religious concerns, immigration, racism and the Ku Klux Klan.

## KEY DATES

**1919** 18th Amendment – introduction of prohibition.
**1921** Presidency of Warren Harding.
   Budget and Accounts Act – to make government spending more accountable.
   Emergency Immigration Act.
**1923** Death of President Harding.
   Ku Klux Klan claim 5,000,000 members.
**1924** Johnson-Reed Immigration Act.
**1925** 'Monkey Trial' – for teaching evolution.
**1927** Execution of Saccho and Vanzetti.

## 1 Introduction

The 1920 Census showed more people living in towns than the countryside for the first time in American history – 54 million out of 106 million Americans (see page 37). However urban areas were defined as those with a population of only 2,500 plus. Moreover, of that 54 million, 16 million still lived in communities of under 25,000 and clung to their rural values such as thrift, hard work and plain living. Tensions in the 1920s were often, but not always, focused between those who lived in rural and small-town America and those who lived in cities, whose ways were seen as wild and sinful. From 1920 to 1930, those living in cities of more than 100,000 increased by a third. Many people saw this growth of urban living as a real threat to what they saw as the American way of life. Their support for the Republican Presidents of the 1920s was part of an effort to turn back the clock.

# 2 The Presidency of Warren Harding

> **KEY ISSUE**  Was Warren Harding's presidency adequate to meet the issues and problems facing the USA in the 1920s?

The 1920 presidential election campaign focused on the issues of Isolationism and a reduced government role. The Republican nominee, Warren Harding was a compromise candidate; he had won his party's nomination only on the ninth ballot of the conference to choose the candidate, when it was clear none of the front runners had enough support to win. To avoid upsetting possible supporters, Harding himself had a minimum of policies – except the proposal to 'return to normalcy' . He meant by this letting the economy run itself, and the government limiting its role. These were the political ideas of the nineteenth century, when, except in times of crisis, the executive was generally weak. His Democrat opponent said much the same things on domestic matters. However, the Democratic party had been hurt by its support for the League of Nations and the European peace treaties. In the event, Harding won the election by 16 million popular votes to 9 million and 404 to 127 electoral college votes.

Harding and Calvin Coolidge, his vice president, were men from small towns who had risen patiently and luckily up the political ladder. For example, Coolidge was a competent but uninspiring governor of Massachusetts who had attracted national fame at a fortuitous time (at the start of the nomination process) by dismissing striking policemen in Boston. By way of contrast, Harding, who bore a remarkable resemblance to George Washington, did actually have the appearance most people imagined a president should have – but he was very aware of his own limitations. 'My God,' he once said, 'this is a hell of a place for a man like me.'

Harding has been regarded until recently as one of the worst American Presidents. He appointed to high office some very dubious characters who later went to prison for corruption. His administration seemed to achieve comparatively little. But it must be remembered that Harding was, in fact, elected to do little – to reduce the role of federal government and to return the USA to 'normalcy'. Some historians have more recently argued that Harding may have been a rather more effective President in some respects than his reputation suggests. Rather than reduce the role of federal government he did, in fact, increase it. He made some sound appointments – Charles Evans Hughes as Secretary of State, Andrew Mellon as Treasury Secretary and Herbert Hoover as Secretary of Commerce. He had promised to cut government expenditure that had risen from $500 million in 1913 to $5,000 million by 1920. In 1921, his government passed the Budget and Accounting Act by which departments had to present their budgets to the President for approval. By 1922, expenditure had fallen to $3,373 million. This gave Mellon the opportunity to reduce taxes; he cut the maximum surtax by 25 per cent and raised tax exemptions. He approved the Sheppard–Towner Maternity Aid Act which gave federal aid to states to develop infant and maternity health programmes and has been seen by some historians as a precedent for later New Deal social legislation. He pressurised US Steel to introduce a basic eight-hour working day. Harding spoke out against racial segregation in Birmingham, Alabama, heartland of the racist South. However, some cynics have argued that he did this primarily to win the electoral support of northern afro-caribbeans. Indeed, one historian has even claimed that Harding was inducted into the Ku Klux Klan in the White House.[1] Certainly he did nothing to oppose the harsh immigration laws.

# 3 Corruption in High Places

> **KEY ISSUE** How did Warren Harding's appointees misuse their power?

After Harding's death in office in summer 1923, several of his appointees were implicated in scandals that had taken place during his time as President.

## a) Charles Forbes

Forbes, the Director of the Veterans' Bureau, was indicted on two main counts; that he had accepted loans from a construction firm bidding for government contracts and that he had sold millions of dollars worth of Bureau supplies at very cheap rates to his business friends. He was fined $10,000 and sent to prison for two years.

## b) Jess Smith and Thomas Miller

Smith was personal secretary to Attorney General Harry Daugherty and Miller was in charge of looking after property taken from nationals of enemy powers. In return for considerable bribes, they upheld the dubious claims of a German banking company to recover $7 billion confiscated during the war. As the evidence came to light, Smith killed himself, while Miller chose to go to jail. The former Attorney General was himself tried on two occasions for his involvement in this and other scandals – he shared a bank account with Smith – but no hard evidence ever came to light.

### c) Albert Fall

The biggest scandal concerned Albert Fall, the Secretary of the Interior, whose salary of $12,000 was scarcely compatible with his lavish spending on his New Mexican ranch. It was discovered that Fall had offered valuable leases to oil companies to drill at Teapot Dome, Wyoming and Elk Hills, California. Both these sites were federal petrol reserves held in trust for the navy. Fall had pressurised the Navy Secretary to transfer their administration to the Interior Department. Again, Fall was given considerable bribes. He was fined $10,000 and went to jail for a year.

## 4 Assessment of Harding's Presidency

> **KEY ISSUE** Does Harding deserve his reputation as an inadequate president?

While Harding was undoubtedly well meaning, the crucial question is whether his presidency was adequate to meet the needs of a changing society. While he made some sound appointments, he also, as we have seen, gave his cronies the chance to line their own pockets. While he did try to make government more efficient – as, for example, with the Budget and Accounting Act – and approved programmes of federal aid, it is difficult to find many other solid achievements in his administration. Nevertheless, despite his advocacy of a return to 'normalcy', he was much more than a do-nothing President. There was at the time considerable concern within Congress about the level of executive involvement in legislation. He called for an increased federal government role in the social and economic life of the nation and addressed Congress no less than six times to put pressure on it to agree to issues he felt strongly about. He was no dynamic, reforming President but he had been elected to reduce, not expand the role of federal government. The very fact that his government achieved as much as it did in the face of prevailing political conditions should be enough to make us reconsider the verdict that Harding was one of the worst American Presidents.

How highly would you rate him as a president?

## 5 Tensions in Society

> **KEY ISSUE** What tensions were present in society and how adequately were they dealt with?

It may be that, for all his good intentions, Warren Harding was simply not up to the job of President in the face of the huge changes taking place in American society. Despite the wishes of many Americans, 'normalcy' could not be restored in the way they hoped – if it had ever existed in the first place: we often view the past through rose-tinted spectacles. While many hoped to return to the days of hardy, God-fearing pioneers, the reality of the past was very different from this image, and, in any event, new conditions in society made such a return impossible. Ironically, with a comparatively weak executive at odds with Congress and with widespread corruption, Harding may indeed have recreated a fairly typical nineteenth-century administration – but this was no longer adequate, if indeed it ever had been so. The USA was changing considerably; it simply was not possible to turn back the clock and certainly not to a time that had existed largely only in mythology. As we shall see, Harding's successor, Coolidge, tried to do the same thing, equally, in the end, without success. Neither understood the tensions that were developing within American society. The 1920s could be seen, in Daniel Snowman's telling phrase, as an age of 'rose coloured nightmares'.[2] There was, on the surface, unbounded optimism exemplified by the growth of the cinema; 'fads' such as sitting on top of flagpoles and mah-jongg; jazz and new and exciting dance crazes; and Charles Lindburgh and the first solo flight across the Atlantic. But if one probed more deeply, real tensions emerged. The truth was that nineteenth-century ideas were largely redundant by the second decade of the twentieth century, despite the fact that many people were trying to hold on to them and feared the new.

## 6 Prohibition

> **KEY ISSUE** What was prohibition and what problems did it cause in American life?

Prohibition was the banning of the manufacture and sale of alcoholic beverages. It illustrates well the contradictions in American society and politics during this period. Supported by those who looked to the government for 'moral regulation' – leading the way to ensure people led clean, wholesome lives – it involved the government interfering in private life to an unprecedented degree. Prohibition was favoured by a variety of interests. Many women's groups saw alcohol as a means by which men oppressed them. Big business saw drunkenness as leading to danger and inefficiency in the workplace – particularly in large factories. Many religious groups believed alcohol was the work of the devil and was overwhelmingly responsible for sin and wrongdoing. Supporters tended to be overwhelmingly Protestant, live in small towns in the South and West and, except in the former region, vote Republican; opponents were likely to be urban, of non-northern European ethnic origin, Roman Catholic and vote Democrat.

It seems almost incredible to us that a nation as large and sophisticated as the USA could even attempt to ban something as commonly available as alcohol; but there was actually surprisingly little opposition to the measure. By 1917, 27 states had already passed prohibition laws and there were 'dry' counties in several others. Two factors led to an increased popularity of prohibition at this time.

## a) The Impact of War

The First World War gave several boasts to prohibition. Grain was needed for food. As a result, many people felt it patriotic to do without a drink. Many of the largest brewers, such as Ruppert, Pabst and Leiber, were of German origin and their businesses had helped finance the National German-American Alliance that had supported German interests before the war. Many people believed sobriety would be part of the 'brave new world' created after the war. It was felt that alcohol led young soldiers away from home for the first time, into temptation and sinful ways – so best to remove it from their grasp.

## b) Disorganisation of the Opposition

The forces against prohibition were not well organised. Beyond a march and rally in New York City, a parade in Baltimore and a resolution against taking away the working man's beer by the American Federation of Labor there was little protest.

In the event, the 18th Amendment, 1919, banned the sale, transportation and manufacture of intoxicating liquor within the USA and the separate Volstead Act defined 'intoxicating liquor' as any drink containing more than half a percent of alcohol. Responsibility for enforcement was given to the Treasury; the first Prohibition Commissioner, John F. Kramer had no doubt his department would be successful:

1 The law will be obeyed in cities, large and small, and in villages, and where it is not obeyed, it will be enforced. ... The law says that liquor to be used as a beverage must not be manufactured. We shall see that it is not manufactured. Nor sold, nor given away, nor hauled in anything
5 on the surface of the earth or under the earth or in the air.

The Anti-Saloon League estimated a $5 million appropriation would be enough; in the event, Kramer's department was given $2 million. This was to be a classic case of a law being passed which it was impossible to enforce. There were six main groups of reasons for this:

i) The USA has 18,700 miles of coastline and land border; those waters just outside the national limits became known, with good reason, as 'rum row'. Smuggling was so successful that in 1925, the officer in charge of prohibition enforcement guessed that agents only intercepted about 5 per cent of alcohol coming into the country illegally; in 1924, they seized $40 million worth of alcohol so the actual volume of business must have been immense.

ii) Chemists could still sell alcohol on doctors' prescriptions; this was naturally open to widespread abuse. Many people known as 'bootleggers' went into business as producers and distributors of illegal alcohol. The 'King of the Bootleggers', George Remus bought up various breweries on the eve of prohibition for the manufacture of medicinal alcohol; he then arranged for an army of 3,000 gangsters to highjack his products and divert them to the illegal stills of the big cities. In five years, Remus made $5,000,000.

iii) Industrial alcohol was easily diverted and re-distilled. Problems with the suitability of this for consumption can easily be imagined and exotic cocktails were often invented to take away the unpleasant smell and taste of materials intended for industrial manufacture. There is a legend that one sceptical buyer took his bootleg whisky for analysis to a chemist – to be told that his horse had diabetes! Poisoning from wood alcohol, though not common, was known during this period and in one instance, 34 people died in New York City.

iv) At the most, 3,000 treasury agents were employed to enforce prohibition. They were paid an average salary of $2,500 to shut down an illegal industry whose profits were estimated at $2 billion annually. It is no wonder that many were corrupt. One federal agent was said to have made $7 million selling illegal licences and pardons to bootleggers. While agents such as 'Izzy' Einstein and 'Moe' Smith became famous for the ingenuity with which they closed down illegal stills and 'speakeasies', it should be remembered that, between 1920 and 1930, about 10 per cent of prohibition agents were fined for corruption. It is very likely that many more escaped prosecution.

v) As the 1920s progressed, the mood of the nation changed. For many Americans, particularly those living in the cities, their main aim in life became having a good time. Illegal drinking in gangster-run 'speakeasies' became popular venues for many fashionable city dwellers.

vi) Against this, the 'dry' lobby, while very well organised to achieve prohibition, was ill equipped to help enforce it. The Anti-Saloon League, for example, was bitterly divided between those who sought stricter enforcement laws, believing the League should actually be given power over appointment of officers, and those who emphasised education programmes to deter people from drinking in the first place.

There is no doubt that prohibition led to a huge growth in crime and gangsterism. Mobsters controlled territories by force and established monopolies of which the huge trusts would have been proud. They could control politicians with ease. The Mayor of Chicago, for example, allowed gangsters such as Al Capone to function unmolested in his city. In 1925 the Mayor was defeated in the election, following the discovery that $1 million had gone missing from public funds. Undaunted, the gangsters simply moved their headquarters to the suburb of Cicero Park until they could get their man elected again.

Al Capone, the most notorious of the gangsters became something of a media star. He saw himself as embodying the spirit of free competition and enterprise in the USA. He saw himself as a businessman who supplied what people wanted. In an age when government, as we shall see, interfered little in business, he seemed not to understand that what he was doing was wrong. He was a fervent Republican despite the fact that – or perhaps because – this was the party of prohibition, and prohibition provided him with his vast profits. When Capone finally went to jail in 1932 – for income tax evasion – it was estimated his gang had done some $70 million worth of business. Capone said:

1 If people didn't want beer and wouldn't drink it, a fellow would be crazy for going around to try to sell it. I've seen gambling houses too ... and I never saw anyone point a gun at a man and make him go in. ... I've always regarded it as a public benefaction if people were given decent
5 liquor and square (honest) games.

By the end of the 1920s, many people questioned whether the 'noble experiment' had been worth it. It had certainly led to an explosion in crime. Between 1927 and 1930 alone, there were 227 gangland murders in Chicago with only two perpetrators ever convicted. Moreover, illegal drinking made criminals of a good percentage of the population. Interestingly, it had been the working-class saloons that tended to be shut down; the 'speakeasies' which replaced them tended to sell spirits to a wealthy clientele; in this respect prohibition worked to the detriment of the poor. Some historians have even argued that Congress did not do more to enforce prohibition because it did not want to alienate rich and influential voters. In addition, this was a period of a reduced role by federal government and most state governments were, at best, lukewarm in enforcement, particularly where cost was concerned. No one in government seemed to be prepared to say openly that prohibition could not be enforced because Americans liked to drink, but this was nevertheless apparent to many people. President Hoover set up the Wickersham Commission to investigate prohibition. When it reported after 19 months' deliberation, its findings were that the law could not be enforced – and yet the Commission as a whole favoured a continuation of prohibition. The New York World mocked the Commission as follows:

1 Prohibition is an awful flop
  We like it
  It can't stop what it's meant to stop
  We like it
5 It's left a trail of graft and slime
  It's filled our land with vice and crime
  It don't prohibit worth a dime
  Nevertheless we're for it.

Prohibition was not finally repealed until 1933, when the 20th Amendment made it the responsibility of individual states to decide on the issue.

# 7 Religion and Morality

> **KEY ISSUE** How did religious and other moral groups respond to the supposed immorality of the period?

Many people associated new ideas, particularly in the cities, with vice and immorality. There was widespread distrust of cinema, jazz music and its associated dances, particularly the Charleston and the Black Bottom. Women who wore short skirts, smoked in public and frequented speakeasies were regarded as shameless. After a series of high profile scandals such as that which destroyed the career of 'Fatty' Arbuckle, a very popular comedy star, the movie industry agreed in 1922 to self-censorship through an office run by Will Hays. This examined every movie made in Hollywood for any immoral content and also attempted to promote clean living among movie stars. There was concern with the growth of crime and fear that it might spread into rural and small-town areas.

These concerns led to something of a revival in religious belief. This 'fundamentalism' involved, among other things, a belief in the literal truth of the Bible and a desire to live one's life according to its teachings. Popular preachers (called evangelists) such as Billy Sunday who preached hellfire and damnation were quick to take advantage of both new marketing techniques, such as radio advertising, and old ones, such as mass rallies. Church figures showed that while people were going to fewer churches, the ones they did patronise were actually growing more popular. This was particularly the case in the cities, possibly as a reaction by God-fearing urbanites against the sinfulness of their neighbourhoods. Aimee Semple McPherson, for example, was an evangelist who ran the Angelus Temple in Los Angeles; it held a congregation of 5,000 and contained a huge tank in which she could baptise 150 people at a time.

However, the real controversy over religion focused on the Scopes Trial of 1925. Fundamentalists had set up an Anti-Evolution League and six states, including Tennessee, had made it illegal for evolution to be taught in schools. John Scopes, a teacher in the small town of Dayton in Tennessee, was persuaded to put the law to the test. He taught evolution, was prosecuted and the ensuing trial became a media event. Prosecuting was the grand old figure of William Jennings Bryan, a former presidential candidate, while Clarence Darrow, one of America's leading liberal lawyers, agreed to lead the defence. During the trial Darrow ridiculed Bryan with his fundamentalist beliefs. The latter admitted to believing that Eve was literally created out of Adam's rib, that the whale swallowed Jonah and that the world was created in 4004 BC. While many urbanites found this hilarious, the small-town jury nevertheless found Scopes guilty and he was fined $100.

# 8 Immigration Laws and Racism

> **KEY ISSUE** How did racism show itself in the USA through responses to the 'Red Scare' and immigration, and the growth of the Ku Klux Klan?

The USA prided itself on being a land born of immigrants. However, this did not prevent there being laws banning the Chinese from entry. The truth was that the USA basically welcomed white immigrants, preferably from north-western Europe. The large-scale waves of immigration from southern and eastern Europe in the latter part of the nineteenth and early twentieth centuries led to racist concerns about the survival of the 'Anglo-Saxon' race. Figures in 1920 showed that 58.5 per cent of the population had native white parents but there was nevertheless considerable racist concern that the Anglo-Saxons were being swamped by 'inferior' races which bred much more quickly. Racist tracts such as 'The Passing of the Great Race' by Madison Grant became best sellers. There were, in addition, dubious tests that seemed to suggest 'Anglo-Saxons' were superior to other races; these seemed to give credence to the ideas promoted by Grant. During the First World War, for example, the Army began to administer Stanford-Binet intelligence tests to new recruits to identify potential officers. However, most of the questions demanded good knowledge of American history and geography, which recent immigrants from southern and eastern Europe tended not to have. The result was that they came out seeming less intelligent than the northern Europeans who tended to have lived in the USA longer and were, therefore, more knowledgeable about its history and geography. Nevertheless, all this was fuel to the racist fire.

## a) The 'Red Scare'

After the First World War, high inflation – in 1920 prices had doubled since 1913 – caused much industrial unrest. It was estimated that during 1919 4,000,000 workers went on strike. This was one in five of the labour force. Many people believed strikers were led by Communists who sought revolution in the USA in the same way that it had been achieved in the USSR. Fears grew as a general strike brought the city of Seattle to a halt and policemen struck in Boston. 340,000 steel workers went on strike. Their leader, William Z Foster was believed to be a Communist. Recent immigrants from Eastern and Southern Europe came, in particular, to be identified with Communism and attempts to overthrow the American system of government. There were, in addition, various assassination attempts on high profile Americans such as John D Rockefeller, the billionaire.

In the period following the First World War and in the wake of the Russian Revolution there was a 'Red Scare' that saw 6,000 arrests. These were known as the 'Palmer Raids', named after the then Attorney General, Mitchell Palmer, himself an intended target for assassination. Palmer had become very popular through his exposure of 'communist activity' in the USA. He hoped he could use this as a springboard for Democratic nomination for the presidency in 1920. In August 1919, Palmer had created the General Intelligence Division to investigate revolutionary activities. Under its head, J Edgar Hoover, this was the forerunner of the Federal Bureau of Investigation (FBI) and Mitchell had relied heavily on its information for his targets. However, most of the detainees had to be released within a few days due to a complete lack of evidence against them. The sweep netted no more than three pistols, while most of those arrested were long-standing US citizens of impeccable respectability. Palmer announced there was to be a huge Communist demonstration in New York on 20 May 1920. When this failed to materialise he increasingly looked ridiculous and the Red Scare died away. With it went his hopes of nomination for the presidency.

However, the case of Saccho and Vanzetti would not go away. They were Italian immigrants, neither of whom spoke English well. When they were arrested carrying out a robbery near Boston in May 1920, they were found to be carrying guns. They also claimed to be Anarchists. Although there was little concrete evidence against them, Saccho and Vanzetti were found guilty and eventually executed in 1927 after years of legal appeals. The case shocked many liberals in the cities, such as the humorist Dorothy Parker who had vigorously protested the innocence of the two. Even though someone else confessed to the crimes for which they had been found guilty, the sentence remained. Protests at their executions led to riot squads being called in to Boston.

However, many in rural America supported the executions. They were coming to believe that cities were filled with 'foreigners' who would not adopt American ways and who were determined to overthrow the American way of life.

## b) Immigration

In 1921 Congress passed an Emergency Immigration Law. This imposed an annual ceiling on immigration from any European country, limiting it to 3 per cent of the nationals from that country living in the USA in 1911. In 1924 this was stiffened by the Johnson–Reed Immigration Act which banned any immigration from

Japan – other Asian groups having been barred earlier – and set an absolute ceiling of immigration at 150,000 per annum, apportioned according to the native origins of the existing white population. This clearly favoured those from north-western Europe. Interestingly, this law did not apply to Mexicans, whom Californian farmers traditionally used as a supply of cheap labour at harvest time.

## c) Ku Klux Klan

Racism meanwhile was widespread, particularly in small towns and rural areas against afro-caribbeans and other non-white groups. The Ku Klux Klan had flourished in the South in the years following the Civil War, where it had terrorised afro-caribbeans and stopped them from taking part in the political process. It was reborn in 1915 as an organisation to promote white supremacy and gained considerable support in the Midwest as well as the South. Using modern business and salesmanship techniques coupled with more brutal methods such as telling members to play on whatever prejudices were most common in their particular area, it had attracted 100,000 followers by 1921. Two of its leaders, Edgar Clark and Elizabeth Tyler, were professional fundraisers and publicity agents. They divided the country into eight 'domains', each under a 'Grand Goblin'. Domains were subdivided into 'realms', each under a 'Grand Dragon', with a bewildering array of minor posts under him – such as Kludds and Kleagles. Recruits were charged $10, most of which went to local Klan officials, and were paid on a commission basis for signing up further new members. The robes, which cost $3.28 to make and sold for $6.50, were manufactured by a Klan-owned clothing company, and all printed material was published at vast profit by the Searchlight Publishing Company, again owned by the Klan. It even moved into land sales through the Clark Realtor Company. All in all, the Klan made a large amount of money out of its members.

The Klan was opposed not just to afro-caribbeanss, but also to Jews, Catholics and foreigners. It attacked new ideas such as evolution and working on the Sabbath. It also opposed any borrowing from non-'Anglo-Saxon' cultures. Undoubtedly the Klan met a need among many Americans. It gave them a sense of importance – particularly those who held local office – belonging and power. With its secretive language, hoods and robes, burning crosses and propensity to violence, it added purpose and glamour to the humdrum lives of the farmers, artisans and shopkeepers who were the mainstay of its membership. Undoubtedly, it also appealed to the bullying and sadistic instincts in many. Victims could be tarred and feathered, branded and even killed. Plain living, prohibition and church attendance could now be upheld by terror. However, despite its apparent success, the Klan was essentially defensive. It was made up of people who were afraid of changes that they neither understood nor had control over.

Hiram Wesley Evans, a Texas dentist, became Imperial Wizard of the Klan on the death of Clark in 1924. He said the Klan was made up of 'plain people, very weak in matters of culture but representing the old pioneer stock, the blend of the nordic races which had given the world its civilisation'. He meant by this whites who saw themselves as the descendants of the people who had settled and civilised the USA and now felt threatened by the emergence of other ethnic and social groups such as Jews, immigrants from southern and eastern Europe, Catholics, and, of course, afro-caribbeans.

The Klan had very little influence in big cities. It was overwhelmingly a movement of small towns and rural areas. There is little doubt that while not all would go to its extremes in terms of violence, many in these areas broadly supported its ideas – and just like the gangsters, the Klan had control of influential politicians. It has been alleged, for example, that in 1924 it helped elect governors in Maine, Ohio, Colorado and Louisiana. At one point both Georgia senators were Klansmen. Certainly it helped destroy the campaign of Al Smith – a Catholic New Yorker – to be nominated for President in 1924, and fought energetically against him again in 1928. Evans claimed there were 5,000,000 members of the Klan in 1923.

However, the Klan rapidly collapsed as a mass organisation. In Indiana, David Stevenson had built the Klan into a powerful political machine. His downfall was sudden and shocking; this followed the suicide of a woman he had raped. He was convicted of second degree murder. Stevenson's wickedness helped kill off large-scale support of the Klan. The organisation was also hurt by revelations of financial mismanagement in Pennsylvania. By 1929, its membership had fallen to 200,000. Evans tried to turn the Klan into more of a social club by emphasising outdoor activities such as camping expeditions as opposed to its political role and attraction to violence. This angered the extremists who felt it had gone soft. By 1930 the power and influence of the Klan was broken on the national stage, although its terrorism continued at local levels.

## 9 The Old Versus the New

> **KEY ISSUE** How do factors such as prohibition, the Red Scare, religion and morality, immigration and the Ku Klux Klan illustrate the tensions in US society?

Many historians have seen these developments – prohibition, fundamentalist religion and racism – as last-ditch attempts by people in small-town and rural America to turn back the tide of the twentieth century. They wanted to keep the USA white, Anglo-Saxon Protestant (WASP). They feared immigrants would shift the racial balance, introduce foreign ideas such as Communism, and overthrow the existing order. Even Roman Catholicism was distrusted, being seen somehow as a threat to American religious practices. They feared alcohol had led to sinfulness and sexual licence in cities, which they saw as hotbeds of vice. They feared afro-caribbeans and the influence of their culture on the young. Above all, they feared change. They believed in a largely imagined past time of hard work, high moral standards of behaviour and unquestioning belief in the literal truth of the Bible.

As with all mythologies, the period to which these people yearned to return had never existed – for all its achievements, the history of the USA had often been turbulent, violent and racist. However, if the 1920s were a volatile decade, many of the problems came to be concealed by a veneer of optimism, excitement, and unparalleled prosperity.

## References

1  S.D. Cashman, *America in the Twenties and Thirties* (New York University Press, 1989), p. 77
2  D. Snowman, *USA, The Twenties to Vietnam* (Batsford, 1968), Chapter 1.

### Summary diagram
Tensions in the 1920s

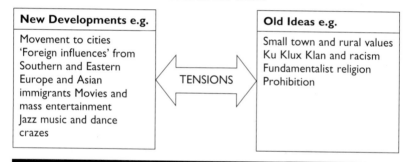

| New Developments e.g. | | Old Ideas e.g. |
|---|---|---|
| Movement to cities 'Foreign influences' from Southern and Eastern Europe and Asian immigrants Movies and mass entertainment Jazz music and dance crazes | TENSIONS | Small town and rural values Ku Klux Klan and racism Fundamentalist religion Prohibition |

## Working on Chapter 2

This chapter has attempted to do two things:

**i)** To consider the presidency of Warren Harding, particularly in terms of whether it was adequate to meet the needs of a changing society (sections 2, 3 and 4).

**ii)** To examine the tensions within society (sections 5, 6, 7, 8 and 9).

### The Presidency of Warren Harding
In making notes on Harding, you could draw up a chart:

| Successes | Failures | Initiatives that came to nothing |
|---|---|---|
|  |  |  |

This should, when completed, help you to draw up a balance sheet for Harding's presidency. You could then go on to examine the scandals of his presidency.

This would enable you finally make a judgement on how adequate a president you think he was.

### Tensions in Society
In considering issues such as Prohibition, religion and morality, immigration, racism and the Ku Klux Klan, it will be useful for you to bear in mind which groups supported and opposed them and how far the tensions can in fact be seen as a small-town and rural USA versus big city divide.

### Prohibition
How well does this illustrate the tensions in American society during this period? What factors led to prohibition? Why did prohibition fail? How was it possible for organised crime to take advantage of prohibition?

### Religion and morality
What concerns led to a growth in fundamentalist religion? How did the Scopes trial show the difference between fundamentalist beliefs and more modern thinking in the USA?

### Immigration and racism
How did immigration lead to concerns about the survival of the Anglo-Saxon race? In what ways were the immigration laws of 1921 and 1924 racist? What was the Ku Klux Klan and sort of people supported it? Why did they do so? Why did the Klan rise and fall so quickly?

### The Old Versus the New
What did those favouring 'old values' fear?

## Answering essay questions on Chapter 2

You would be unlikely to face a question purely on the presidency of Warren Harding. However, questions dealing collectively with the three Republican Presidents of the period – Warren Harding (1921–3), Calvin Coolidge (1923–9) and Herbert Hoover (1929–33) – are quite common and will be tackled at the end of Chapter 5.

From reading this chapter you should be able to tackle questions on social issues such as Prohibition and the Ku Klux Klan.

### Prohibition
Essays on this subject are common. They take several forms, for example:

I. Why was prohibition not successful?

The key word in this essay is, of course, 'successful'. In order to tackle it, you need to consider the problems with the enforcement of prohibition and how it led to social problems such as the rise of gangsterism. In conclusion, it is worth considering why governments persisted with 'the noble experiment' until 1933 even though it was fairly obvious to most people that it had failed.

A more specific type of question is:

**2.** Account for the early success and later failure of the Prohibition campaign. To tackle this question you will need firstly to examine the reasons for the passage of prohibition into law. The second part invites you to examine its subsequent problems, leading to a discussion of why it failed. In questions such as this, with two parts, examiners almost always divide the marks equally so you have to tackle each part equally well.

### Ku Klux Klan
Essay questions on the Ku Klux Klan might ask you to:

**1.** Account for the rise and fall of the Ku Klux Klan in the 1920s.
Here you will need to examine why the Klan was so popular. Consider its policies; its marketing; and the apparent excitement it offered people in rural and small-town USA. You can then go on to why it failed; the scandal of Stevenson and internal corruption among its leadership will figure largely here.

**2.** How did the Klan affect American society in the 1920s.?
The focus here is on the Klan's policies and where they were influential. You need to write about its success in small-town and rural USA and lack of influence in the cities where there was more of an ethnic mix. You could examine its policies in terms of racism, religion and simple lifestyles. You might look at how it controlled some politicians in the early 1920s but how its popularity subsequently declined.

You could also, more likely in the second year of 'A' level, find questions on the rural-urban divide.

**3.** 'The revolt of rural and small-town USA against the cities.' Discuss this view of the 1920s.
You need to be very careful when tackling questions of this nature as they can lend themselves to vagueness in your answers. You need to be quite precise in what content to include. You could, for example, look at prohibition, fundamentalist religion, attitudes to immigration and racism, and discuss how far each of these factors was supported by those who lived in small towns and rural areas. You could then go on to discuss what developments in cities these groups particularly disliked and the reasons for this dislike. You do not have to agree with the quotation; but you must in your conclusion arrive at a judgement that would be supported by what you have written. It is vital to support your argument with evidence – to sustain your judgements.

## Source-based questions on Chapter 2

### 1. Prohibition

Read carefully the extract by John F. Kramer on page 13, by Al Capone on page 15, and the satirical poem on page 15. Answer the following questions.

**a)** What can you learn from the extracts by Al Capone and the New York World about the reasons why prohibition failed? *(3 marks)*

**b)** Use your own knowledge to explain why prohibition was introduced into the USA in 1919. *(5 marks)*

**c)** Assess the usefulness of the sources by John F. Kramer and Al Capone to an historian studying prohibition. *(6 marks)*

**d)** Do the extracts by Al Capone and the New York World agree with or contradict the extract by John F. Kramer? Explain your answer carefully. *(6 marks)*

**e)** Using the arguments contained in these extracts and your own knowledge, explain why prohibition failed. *(10 marks)*

Some source-based questions will ask for your own knowledge. Here the sources are intended as a stimulus only and you will not be awarded any marks for using them in your answer. Where you are asked to use both the sources and your own knowledge, half the marks allocated will probably be available for each – so, if you ignore either the sources or your own knowledge in your answer, at most you will get half the marks allowed.

Often source-based questions begin with comprehension-type questions carrying just a few marks. They go on to ask you to evaluate the evidence and compare extracts. In these types of questions, examiners are looking to see that you do not use the sources simply for information. Higher level answers can place sources in context, discuss issues such as origin, reliability and purpose, with extracts judiciously cited to support their answers.

When answering the questions about usefulness above, you should show that, as Prohibition Commissioner, John F. Kramer wanted to reassure the American people that prohibition was going to be enforced, although the source was written before it had begun and before the problems in relation to it had come to the surface. Al Capone is seeking to justify himself, and, although it gives his point of view, cannot be taken as evidence of what really happened.

# 3 Prosperity?

## POINTS TO CONSIDER

When reading this chapter, you need to consider three issues: what sort of president was Calvin Coolidge; why was the USA apparently so prosperous in the 1920s; and how real and widespread was this apparent prosperity?

## KEY DATES

**1921** Emergency Tariff Act.
**1922** Fordney–McCumber Act – raising of tariffs.
**1923** Presidency of Calvin Coolidge.
Agricultural Credit Act – credit banks funded to offer loans to farming co-operatives.
**1924** McNary–Haugen Bill first debated – government help for agriculture.
**1926** End of the Florida Land Boom.

## 1 The New President

**KEY ISSUE** What sort of president was Calvin Coolidge?

On 2 August 1923 Warren Harding died. His vice-president, Calvin Coolidge was visiting his family in his home state of Vermont at the time. Coolidge was duly sworn in as 30th President of the United States by his father, a local lawyer, in the kitchen of the family homestead in the tiny hamlet of Plymouth Notch. This action was in fact unnecessary. John Coolidge had not the authority to swear in a new president, and in any event his son automatically succeeded Harding as chief executive. However, the gesture did set the tone for Coolidge's presidency. He liked to be thought of as a man of and from the people – particularly those of small-town America whose values included hard work, thrift, looking after their own and not expecting the government to bail them out in times of trouble.

Coolidge was honest and decent. He had a strong sense of personal morality. Unlike his predecessor, there were no scandals attached to him. Quiet and shy, 'Silent Cal' established an indolent routine in the White House. He enjoyed a nap most afternoons and it was always early to bed in the evening. Official functions were known to end prematurely if they were due to go on past his usual bedtime. However, he was rarely burdened with affairs of state. He tired easily and his work-rate was slow. He once said, 'If you see ten troubles coming down the road, you can be sure that nine will run into the ditch and you will only have to battle with one'. Critics said he failed even to do that. Coolidge certainly believed that a good government should do as little as possible. It should at best help things to run themselves.

In his first address to Congress as President in 1923 Coolidge did acknowledge that the USA had problems. He spoke of issues such as lynching, child labour and the need for a minimum wage for women. He recognised the difficulties farmers were in. However, the substance of his message was concerned with tax reductions and economy in government. As President, he would do less, not more, than his predecessors.

He was essentially a man of the nineteenth century whose views were outdated when he came to office. The USA was undergoing dramatic social and economic changes that he quite failed to understand and his way of governing was effectively that of the previous century.

Historians have generally criticised Coolidge and have seen him as one of the weakest of American Presidents. However, this is not how many viewed him at the time. 'Silent Cal' made more speeches and saw more people than any other President before him. He courted publicity and liked to be photographed in outlandish costumes such as Native American head-dress. But his face always seemed to bear the same dry expression, as though he was bemused by and slightly superior to all that was going on around him. He was popular. He represented all those Americans, particularly from 'Middle America', who wanted to enjoy the prosperity unfettered by government regulation, but who still sought to maintain high moral standards in society. There is little doubt that had Coolidge chosen to run for a second full term as President in 1928, he would easily have been re-elected. He gave off an aura of confidence. He was always calm and unflappable. Most people felt there could not be much wrong with the USA with such a dependable pilot at the helm. In one of his last messages to Congress he said:

1  In the domestic field there is tranquility and contentment, harmonious
   relationships between management and the wage earner, freedom from
   industrial strife, and the highest record of years of prosperity. The
   country can regard the present with satisfaction and anticipate the
5  future with optimism.

Many agreed. Calvin Coolidge presided over the largest boom period in American history. Many Americans did not want their government to do much. They believed that they had never been so well off and that the prosperity they enjoyed was permanent. Calvin Coolidge, they felt, had done a fine job as their President.

# 2 The Boom Years

> **KEY ISSUE**  What is the evidence of widespread prosperity and how reliable is it?

In popular mythology, the 1920s in the USA saw a period of unparalleled economic prosperity which ended suddenly in October 1929 with the collapse of the New York Stock Exchange. This picture is far too simplistic. There certainly was a boom period and the New York Stock Exchange did indeed collapse. However, the relationship between these two events is a complex one to unravel.

Following a brief post-war recession in 1920 and 1921, average unemployment never rose above 3.7 per cent in the years 1922 to 1929. Inflation never rose higher than 1 per cent. Employees were working fewer hours – an average of 44 per week in 1929 compared with 47 in 1920. They were paid more. The real wages of industrial workers rose by 14 per cent between 1914 and 1929 and on average they were two or three times higher than those in Europe. There was huge economic growth. Production of industrial goods rose by 50 per cent between 1922 and 1929. Gross National Product (GNP) stood at $73 billion in 1920 and $104 billion in 1929. Consumption of electricity doubled and in 1929 alone $852 million worth of radios were sold.

Many Americans had more time for leisure and more money to spend on it. Electrical labour-saving devices such as vacuum cleaners and washing machines were introduced and became affordable by more and more people. Motor cars made possible greater mobility both to and from work and for leisure pursuits. It was the golden age of cinema – by 1929, 80 million tickets were sold weekly for the movies. When Gene Tunney defended his heavyweight boxing title against Jack Dempsey in September 1927, the attendance was 107,943 and receipts were a record $2,658,660.

However, one must beware aggregate figures and specific examples that support them. They might give us an overall picture but they cannot tell us about individual circumstances. For example, the unemployment figure cannot tell us whether the low figure was general to all sectors of the economy or whether some industries suffered high or seasonal unemployment. Were employees just part-time? What could they buy with their wages? Was the overall prosperity spread throughout the nation or was it principally located in specific parts of the country? Did it apply to all ethnic groups? How did women fare? To answer questions such as these requires more specific evidence.

In the first part of this chapter the apparent economic successes of the decade and the reasons behind them will be discussed, and then the problems surrounding the topic will be considered. This approach should enable an informed judgement to be made about how far the period of the 1920s was, in fact, one of real prosperity.

# 3 Reasons for Prosperity

KEY ISSUE  What were the reasons for the apparent prosperity?

## a) Government Policies

According to Calvin Coolidge, 'The chief business of the American people is business'. It was the policy of his government to let business operate as far as possible free of regulation. Both he and his Treasury Secretary, Andrew Mellon, believed firmly in the free market. Mellon, a Pittsburgh banker and industrialist, was one of the richest men in the USA. He believed that wealth filtered down naturally to all classes in society; that the best way to ensure increased living standards for all was to do everything possible to enable the rich to continue to make money to invest in industrial development. There appeared to be much sense to this argument. Industrial expansion meant more job opportunities which in turn meant more employment, more wage earners, more consumption, more industrial expansion and so on. During the 1920s this policy seemed to work and Mellon had few critics at the time.

The basic government policy was laissez-faire. Strictly speaking, this means that the economy was left to run itself. However, the picture was not quite as simple as that, and the government did intervene to support business with benevolent policies in three main ways.

### i) High Tariffs

The Fordney–McCumber Act, passed in 1922, raised tariffs to cover the difference between domestic and foreign production costs. In effect, this meant that for some products import duties were so high that domestic producers were given an almost guaranteed market. Throughout the 1920s the general level of tariffs was upwards. The level of foreign trade was obviously reduced by this, while domestic demand for goods remained high. American industry stood to make huge profits from the high tariff policy. It, of course, meant that Americans bought comparatively few foreign goods.

### ii) Tax Reductions

The government reduced federal taxes significantly in 1924, 1926 and 1928. These reductions mainly benefited the wealthy. In 1920 the highest surtax stood at 65 per cent; in 1928 this was down to 25 per cent. During his eight years of office, Mellon handed out tax reductions totalling $3.5 billion to large-scale industrialists and corporations. Despite this, Coolidge's government actually operated on a surplus; in 1925, this was $677 million and in 1927, $607 million. The avowed aim of the government was to reduce the National Debt, and it seemed on course to do so. However, of course, federal tax cuts meant little to people who were too poor to pay taxes in the first place.

### iii) Fewer Regulations

Economies in government meant fewer regulations and fewer personnel to enforce them. The Federal Trade Commission, for example, was increasingly unable and unwilling to operate effectively. This trend meant that businesses were often left unhindered to carry on their affairs as they saw fit. Laws concerning sharp business practice, such as price fixing, were often ignored. Where the government did prosecute, the offenders usually won on appeal. This lack of regulation could be an important contributor to a company's profits. While many people welcomed less government, it should also be remembered that there was, for example, no body with the authority to stop child labour in the textile mills of the South, where a 56-hour week was common and wages rarely rose to more than 18 cents an hour.

## b) Technical Advances

During this period great technical advances in industrial production made possible huge increases both in the quantity and in the variety of products on sale. While this is true of almost every type of commodity, the motor vehicle industry and electrical consumer goods will be considered as being particularly typical examples.

### i) Motor Vehicle Industry

Henry Ford revolutionised the motor vehicle industry. He had begun to use methods of mass production long before the 1920s and his famous 'Model T' car had first appeared in 1909. Previously, cars had been only for the wealthy, but Ford wanted anyone earning a reasonable income to be able to afford one. When he introduced his moving line assembly in 1914, the cost of the Model T came down from $950 to $500. By 1920 Ford could produce 1,250,000 cars per year, or one every 60 seconds. By 1925, when the price had fallen to $290, his factory could produce one every 10 seconds. By this time, Ford was facing increasing competition from General Motors and Chrysler. These 'Big Three' firms dominated the American motor industry and it was very difficult for independent companies to survive unless they produced specialist vehicles for the wealthy. In 1930, 26.5 million cars were on American roads. Despite the demand, the supply always exceeded it, and in this industry as in many others it was increasingly obvious that demand must be actively encouraged. Ford was slow to learn this lesson. His Model T was renowned for durability and trust-worthiness. While it is by no means certain that Ford ever said that the customer could have a Model T in any colour he liked so long as it was black, there was in reality no choice. The car came without frills. It was certainly adaptable; farmers could even attach a plough to it. However, his rivals emphasised variety, comfort and style. When, in 1927, Ford noticeably began to lose his share of the market, he closed down his factory, laying off 60,000 workers. During this layoff, the factory was retooled for the new Model A vehicle. Car design had to stay ahead of the market and customers had to want to buy the new model rather than keep the old one if the market was to remain buoyant.

The growth of the motor industry had major social and economic effects. Henry Ford, with his limited imagination, had seen the car as strengthening what he saw as traditional American values. The family would bond together through outings, the breadwinners could go farther afield to seek work, and so on. He did not forsee its use by courting couples nor did he realise family outings might take the place of church attendance. He had no idea that road deaths would stand at 20,000 per year by the later 1920s, or indeed that the industrial organisation would stimulate the trade unionism which he loathed and forcefully kept out of his own factory. In economic terms, by 1929, the industry employed 7 per cent of all workers and paid them 9 per cent of all wages. By far the largest industry in the USA, it also stimulated many others as may be seen by studying the graph below. This shows the percentages of the total production of various items in the USA which were used by the car industry alone. The temporary closure of Ford was indeed a contributory factor to the recession of 1927.

Breaking with the policy of laissez-faire, the federal government expended a great deal of energy on road building in the 1920s. Until 1921 this had largely been the responsibility of the states and many had made little progress since the previous century. Of 3 million miles of road in 1920, the vast majority were intended solely for the horse. Only about 1 per cent of roads were suitable to take the pounding of motor vehicles. The horse was by far the main form of road transport and the quantity of its dung on the highways was felt to be a national health hazard. The Federal Highway Act of 1921 gave responsibility for road building to central government and highways were being constructed at the rate of 10,000 miles per year by 1929. But this was not enough. New roads could not keep pace with the growth of traffic. Congestion was common, particularly in the approaches to large urban centres. In 1936 the Chief Designer in the Bureau of Public Roads reported that between 25 per cent and 50 per cent of modern roads built over the previous 20 years were unfit for use because of the great demand.

Motor vehicles also created the growth of new service industries such as garages, motels, petrol stations, and used car sale-rooms. They gradually changed the landscape alongside the highways of the USA.

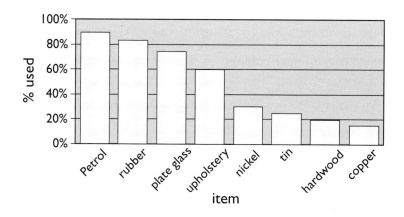

Use of products by the car industry

Improved transportation also afforded new opportunities for industry. For example, goods could be much more easily moved from factories to their markets. The number of truck registrations increased from less than 1 million in 1919 to 3.5 million by 1929, when 15 billion gallons of petrol were used and 4.5 million new cars were sold.

### ii) Electrical Consumer Goods

New technologies facilitated the development of labour-saving devices on a large scale. In 1912, 2.4 million items of electrical goods were sold; in 1929 the figure was 160 million. However, one should beware exaggerating this trend. Despite the efforts of entrepreneurs such as Samuel Insull, much of rural America was still without electricity in the 1920s. Even where electrical power was available, many items we take for granted today were not widely in use. In 1925, for example, Clarence Birdseye patented his freezing process but in 1928 there were only 20,000 refrigerators in the whole country. It would be unrealistic to speak of a 'domestic consumer revolution' during this period unless you are very careful to define exactly what you mean by it.

## c) New Business Methods

This was a period that saw the growth of huge corporations, of scientific methods of management, and of advertising, which through the exploitation of the new mass media, gained an influence previously unimagined.

### i) Growth of Huge Corporations

Large corporations could invest in and exploit the plentiful raw materials of the USA on a vast scale. By 1929 the largest 200 corporations possessed 20 per cent of the nation's wealth and 40 per cent of the business wealth. Mergers in manufacturing and mining concerns trebled to over 1,200 during the decade. Large corporations could dominate an industry in various ways. They could operate a cartel to fix prices. Although this was technically illegal, the government tended to turn a blind eye. They could, as in the case of the petroleum companies, control the entire industrial process from the exploitation of the raw materials, manufacture of the product, distribution to wholesale and retail outlets, to the sale of products to the consumer. Some concerns, for example US Steel, were so huge that they could dictate output and price levels throughout the industry. They could create holding companies. One huge company would obtain a controlling interest in smaller companies to control the market. For example, Samuel Insull built up a vast empire based on electrical supply. Eventually he controlled 111 different companies with as many as 24 layers between him and the company actually distributing the electricity. The chain became so complex that even he lost an overall understanding of it. Many businessmen turned up on the boards of directors of numerous companies, with the effect that firms ostensibly competing with each other were in effect one and the same, with the power to fix output and prices.

It is important to remember that government policies made these developments possible and that they acted against the interests of small businesses. However, at the time many people saw businessmen as heroes who had made possible the great boom period they were enjoying. There was even a prayer especially for businessmen:

1  God of businessmen, I thank Thee for the fellowship
   of red blooded men with songs in their hearts and handclasps that are
   sincere;
   I thank Thee for telephones and telegrams that link
5  me with home and office, no matter where I am.
   I thank Thee for the joy of the battle of the business
   arena, the thrill of victory and the courage to
   take defeat like a good sport;
   I thank Thee for children, friendship, books, fishing,
10 the game of golf, my pipe and the open
   fire on a chilly evening.                                    AMEN

## ii) Management Science

The increased complexity of business management led to the development of different tasks done by different people in administration. Entrepreneurs like Henry Ford who tried to control all management operations were increasingly old fashioned. Specialisms developed in production, design, marketing, accounts and finance in ways that had been unheard of in the previous century. One noticeable aspect of these developments was the growth of business schools – in 1928

there were 89 of them, with 67,000 students. The fact that management science became a respectable occupation for members of the
upper middle classes was also an indication that it was becoming
increasingly difficult to start one's own company. To rise up the
ladder of an established giant offered greater career opportunities
than to compete with them.

Many new 'scientific' management theories were put into operation, particularly the 'time and motion' work of Frederick W. Taylor
and his followers. Levels of production undoubtedly increased, but in
extreme cases all initiative was removed from the labour force, which
tended to become simply extensions of the machine – this development was satirised memorably in Charlie Chaplin's 1936 film, Modern
Times. However, it should be remembered that these developments
applied almost exclusively to large business concerns. Outside the big
cities most manufacturers still worked in small workshops.

### iii) Advertising and Salesmanship
The new mass media, principally cinema and radio, effected a revolution in advertising.

By 1928 there were 17,000 cinemas in the USA. Few areas were out
of the reach of the 'movies'. A 10 cent ticket could buy admission to
a fantasy world far beyond the previous experience of the vast
majority of the audience. The darkened auditorium enabled people
to forget their troubles for a few hours and to enter into a world of
beauty and glamour where seemingly no one had to work or pay the
mortgage.

With millions of cinema-goers aching to copy the appearances and
lifestyles of the stars, the potential for advertising was enormous. The
big producers were not slow to exploit this, and the time between the
features was soon filled with commercials.

The radio business effectively began when the KDKA station in
Pittsburgh announced the results of the 1920 presidential election. As
other stations started to broadcast, a demand for radio sets was
created. These began to be mass produced in 1920 after the end of a
dispute over patents between the main producers. By 1929 there were
618 radio stations throughout the USA, some of them broadcasting
from coast to coast. The vast majority of them were controlled by two
companies, the National Broadcasting Company and Columbia
Broadcasting System. The potential audience was vast. An estimated
50,000,000 people listened to live commentary on the Dempsey-
Tunney fight referred to on page 27. In 1922 WEAF in New York
began the most important trend when it broadcast the first sponsored
programme, advertising the delights of Jackson Heights, a housing
development. As more advertisers began to sponsor programmes,
radio networks began to poll listeners to see what sort of programmes
they wanted. With more and more programmes catering to mass
appeal which was based firmly in the areas of light music and humour,

there was considerable criticism from those who felt radio should be uplifting and enlightening. However, they were firmly in the minority. By the end of the decade, radio costs were generally covered by advertising and many programmes were firmly linked in people's minds with the name of the sponsor.

The growth in industrial production needed a continuous market. It was no longer enough, as Ford had done with his Model T, to sell a durable unchanging product so that one item might last the purchaser for life. Now, to fuel the boom, it was necessary for people to buy new things frequently. They had to be convinced that they could not do without the latest model of an electrical appliance or the new design in clothing. This necessitated far-reaching developments in advertising and salesmanship. Indeed with most types of different goods virtually the same in quality, these often became the variables in the market. A successful advertising campaign might well be the only difference between huge profit and huge loss. Possibly the most important aspect of a campaign was to find some way to differentiate between one's product and that of one's competitors – to promote a unique selling point.

Here are two examples from motor car brochures:

> 1 Packard Luxury is mental no less than physical. The feeling is complete
> security born of easy control, safe steering and effortless braking is a
> luxury. So is the assurance of brilliant and trustworthy performance –
> and pride in a universally acclaimed, unchanging beauty of design and
> 5 color. Nothing in the world is finer. That knowledge is perhaps the
> greatest luxury of all.

> 1 In the automotive world, it is not enough that cars be colorful. They
> should be colored as nature paints. The deep green of the forest is
> peaceful, cheerful, refreshing. It invites to relaxation, to whole hearted
> enjoyment of the hour.
> 5 Cadillac

One of the pioneers of high-pressure salesmanship was Bruce Barton who tried to show that consumer society and the accumulation of wealth was in no way incompatible with Christian teaching. In a series of books such as A Young Man's Jesus (1914) and The Man Nobody Knew (1926), Barton tried to show that Christ himself was a high-pressure salesman:

> 1 He thought of his life as business. What did he mean by business? To
> what extent are the principles by which he conducted his business simi-
> lar to ours? Manufacturers; presidents of railroads and steamship
> companies; the heads of banks and investment houses – all tell the same
> 5 story. 'Service is what we are here for,' they exclaim. They call it the
> 'spirit of modern business'; they suppose, most of them, that it is some-.
> thing very new. But Jesus preached it more than nineteen hundred years
> ago.

For many people advertising techniques worked. Not only did they associate products with a slogan, but they also believed they could not manage without the product being advertised. The Kansas City Journal-Post was hardly exaggerating when it wrote, 'Advertising and mass production are the twin cylinders that keep the motor of modern business in motion'.

## d) Easy Credit

The massive consumer boom was financed largely by easy credit facilities. By 1929 almost $7 billion worth of goods were sold on credit; this included 75 per cent of cars and half of major household appliances. The Lunds' pioneering sociological study of 'Middletown' – in fact, Muncie, Indiana – showed that men earning $35 a week were paying the same amount per month for the family car. A popular joke went:

> Husband: 'I just paid the doctor ten dollars on his bill.'
> Wife: 'Oh, goody, two more payments and the baby's ours.'

The point is, of course, that while credit facilities enabled consumers to buy goods they otherwise could not have afforded, there were potential problems if they over-committed themselves or if their financial circumstances altered. Companies, as well as individuals, used easy credit facilities to finance many of their operations. It seemed that almost everyone was in debt but there was little concern over this. It was assumed that everyone's credit must be good. Banks and loan companies seemed to be falling over backwards to lend money, often with few questions asked.

It seemed in the 1920s that with almost full employment, low inflation, high tariffs keeping foreign goods out of the USA, benevolent government policies and a consumer boom, the prosperity would go on forever. The period was a time of great optimism. It wore a happy face. However, one did not have to delve very far beneath the surface to discover real problems within the system.

# 4  Problems in the Economy

| KEY ISSUE  What was wrong with the economy in the 1920s? |
| --- |

## a) Uneven Distribution of Income

The old industries of the USA had been centred in the North East and Midwest, especially in the states of Illinois, Michigan and Pennsylvania. These had grown originally on the basis of nineteenth-century technology, powered by coal and steam. The new industries such as the motor vehicle and electrical industries were also drawn to these regions. This was due to the availability of minerals such as coal, the well-established transport network, a mobile, often immigrant labour force, and proximity to centres of large population, such as Boston, Philadelphia and New York. As a result, other regions of the USA, notably the West and the South, had only sparse industrial development, with comparatively small towns still acting as magnets for wide hinterlands. Things had not, in other words, altered in much of the USA since the previous century, and for much of the country the major occupation was still agriculture.

Old industries were generally experiencing hard times. Coal, for example, suffered from competition from newly discovered energy sources, notably oil. The introduction of synthetic fibres had adverse effects on the demand for cotton. Moreover, this was at a time when changes, particularly in young women's fashions, dramatically reduced the quantity of material required. The textile mills of the South employed cheap labour, including children, and many northern mills, whose workforce enjoyed higher wages and shorter hours of work, simply could not compete in a shrinking market. Railways faced competition from motor transport – although it must be said that due to the expansion of the economy, rail freight traffic increased 10 per cent during the decade. Farmers fared particularly badly during this period.

One major effect of this disparity in industrial development was that income was distributed very unevenly throughout the country. The North East and Far West enjoyed the highest per capita incomes; in 1929 these were $921 and $881 respectively. In comparison, the figure for the South East was $365. To paint an even gloomier picture, in South Carolina, while the per capita income for the non-agricultural sectors of the economy averaged $412, that of farmers was only $129. In 1929 the Brookings Institute found that income distribution was actually becoming more unequal. Its survey discovered that 60 per cent of American families had annual incomes of less than $2,000. Indeed, in 'Middletown' the Lynds sampled one hundred families and discovered that 75 per cent earned less than the amount the Federal Bureau of Labour recommended as the minimum income needed to support an acceptable standard of living.[1]

In addition, employment was often transitory. The Lynds found that, during the first 9 months of 1924, of 165 families they surveyed, 72 per cent had lost time through unemployment. Of these 43 per cent had been jobless for over a month. This was at a time when there was very little welfare or unemployment benefit and most relief was supplied by charitable organisations.

Women did not on the whole enjoy improved career opportunities during this period. By 1930, for example, there were only 150 women dentists and less than 100 female accountants in the whole of the USA. Women tended to remain in comparatively low-paid and often menial jobs; 700,000 women were domestic servants. There were few female industrialists or managing directors. The number of women receiving a college education actually fell by 5 per cent during the decade. Even when women worked in the same job as men, they normally received less money. Despite the image of 'the flapper', women were generally expected to concentrate on marriage and homemaking. The 'emancipation of women' in terms of employment opportunities during this period is largely a myth.

At the bottom of the pile were Native Americans and afro-caribbeans. Native Americans often eked out a miserable existence on infertile reservations. Afro-caribbeans made up 10 per cent of the total population, but 85 per cent still lived in the South, itself the poorest region in the USA. There was considerable migration north, particularly to the large cities, but here too afro-caribbeans faced discrimination in housing and employment. Increasingly too they were concentrated in 'ghetto' areas such as Harlem in New York, whose afro-caribbean population had swelled from 50,000 in 1914 to 165,000 in 1930. Here overcrowding and poor living conditions added to their problems in the mainstream economy. Peter Gottleib has shown in Pittsburgh that afro-caribbeans were kept unskilled and forced to operate in the casual labour market.[2] This left them more exposed to joblessness and fears of destitution than before they had begun their migration north. In the Midwest and much of the South, the Ku Klux Klan terrorised afro-caribbeans, although the number of lynchings was falling. Comparatively few afro-caribbeans were allowed to share in any prosperity; 14 per cent of farmers were afro-caribbeans.

## b) Farmers

For the first time, the Census showed in 1920 that the USA was essentially an urban nation. The total population was 106,466,000; of these 31,614,000 lived in 6,518,000 farming units, but the rest lived in towns. The growth of urbanisation was particularly significant because farming had been extremely strong in American life and culture. Not only did farmers produce food, the lifeblood of the nation, but they had also given the USA much of its perceived national character – hard work, self-reliance, and overcoming adversity through one's own efforts. The farmers were, in mythology, the people who had tamed and civilised a wilderness. As the majority of Americans had traditionally lived in rural areas, the farmers' lobby in government was very powerful.

The years preceding the 1920s had been relatively good ones for farmers. During the war years prices had risen 25 per cent, and more and more land had been taken into cultivation. However, after the war falling demand led to falling prices. For example, wheat fell from $2.5 to $1 per bushel. There were several reasons for this. Prohibition cut the demand for grain previously used in the manufacture of alcohol, and higher living standards meant Americans ate more meat and fewer cereals. The growth of synthetic fibres lessened the market for

Photograph of rural poverty in Arkansas

natural ones, such as cotton. At the same time, technical advances meant that more could be produced on the same or even a reduced acreage. During the 1920s, 13 million acres were taken out of production and the farm population fell by 5 per cent – yet farm output grew by 9 per cent. Greater use of tractors meant fewer horses were necessary and this in turn meant less demand for animal food. Ironically, because many farmers became more efficient through mechanisation and new techniques such as the use of improved fertilisers and better animal husbandry, they simply produced too much. As a result, possibly as many as 66 per cent of farms operated at a loss. Wage labourers, tenant farmers, and share croppers – in the South, these were mainly afro-caribbeans – fared particularly badly.

Many farmers blamed the government for their plight. During the war, it had urged them to produce more but now it did little to compensate them for their losses. Many farmers were particularly angered by the fact that tariffs protected industry but not agriculture. However, although the farm lobby was very powerful, it was inevitable that if the USA was to continue to develop as an industrial nation, manpower and resources would have to be shifted from agriculture. But economic truths are little comfort to those adversely affected by them – people who may have to leave their homes, their families, everything they know – and the farming lobby fought a valiant rearguard action. However, agriculture would have to change – and change it did.

The concept of the small-scale, self-reliant farmer had already largely become a myth. In order to survive in the long term, farmers needed to make a profit. The 1920s saw the growth of 'agricultural businesses' – highly capitalised cereal cultivation, ranching and fruit production enterprises – using the techniques of mass production. They required comparatively little labour, except possibly in the case of fruit production at harvest time. It was mainly the small-scale farmers who went bankrupt. These often asked the state for help, as they thought of big business and the banks as being in league against them. Government policy was to encourage farms to co-operate together to market their produce. To this end the Agricultural Credits Act of 1923 funded 12 Intermediate Credit Banks to offer loans to co-operatives. However, the measure was of little benefit to small farmers. The last thing they needed was more debt. But agri-businesses did take advantage of them, thus squeezing the small farmers even more.

Two measures of the early 1920s did in theory protect farmers from foreign competition: the 1921 Emergency Tariff Act and the 1922 Fordney–McCumber Act placed high tariffs on food imports. However, because foreigners retaliated by placing similar tariffs on American foodstuffs, farmers could not export their surpluses.

The biggest problem for farmers was overproduction. Too much food meant prices were too low. Farmers would not voluntarily under-produce because they could not trust their neighbours to do the same. Ideally they sought guaranteed prices, with the state possibly selling their surpluses abroad for whatever price it could get. In 1924 the McNary–Haugen bill was proposed in Congress. By its terms an Agricultural Export Corporation would be set up to buy commodities on the American market to sell abroad. Farmers who participated would pay an 'equalisation fee' on each unit sold to cover the difference between the domestic price and the lower foreign prices. But at least it would be guaranteed that they would sell all their produce. In the event, in its final form, the bill transferred the equalisation fee from the farmers to the transportation and processing companies. It passed twice through Congress, only to be vetoed by Coolidge, in a rare burst of energy, on each occasion. The President opposed the measure for three reasons: because it failed to address the overall question of overproduction; because he felt that dumping American food abroad would sour foreign relations; and because he thought it would create the bureaucratic nightmare of attempting to co-ordinate the work of thousands of businesses. In any event the bill was based on two very shaky assumptions: that higher prices would not stimulate additional domestic production; and that foreign markets would actually remain open to American surpluses.

The measure was totally against the principles of Coolidge's government.

1 Instead of undertaking to secure a method of orderly marketing which
  will dispose of products at a profit, it proposes to dispose of them at a
  loss. It runs counter to principles of conservatism which would require
  us to produce only what can be done at a profit not to waste our soil
5 and resources producing what is to be sold at a loss to us for the benefit of the foreign consumer.

Although there was much sense in his arguments, Coolidge did little
to relieve farmers from their distress. More and more saw their mortgages foreclosed and lost land their families had farmed for gener-
ations. Many farmers naturally became very bitter.

Emil Loriks was a State Senator in South Dakota from 1927 to
1934:

1 During my first session in the state senate in 1927 five hundred farmers
  came marching up Capitol Hill. It thrilled me. I didn't know farmers
  were intelligent enough to organise.
  They stayed there for two days. It was a strength I didn't realise we had
5 ... Oh the militancy then! At Millbank, during a farm sale, they had a
  sheriff and sixteen deputies. One of them got a little trigger happy. It
  was a mistake. The boys disarmed him so fast he didn't know what had
  happened. They just yanked the belts off 'em, didn't even bother to
  unbuckle 'em. They took their guns away from 'em. After that we didn't
10 have much trouble stopping sales. The judge situation in Iowa was a
  warning. In Brown County, farmers would crowd into the courtroom,
  five or six hundred, and make it impossible for the officers to carry out
  the sales. Deputies would come along with whole fleets of trucks and
  guns. One lone farmer had planks across the road. They ordered him
15 to remove them. They came out with guns. He said, 'Go ahead and
  shoot, but there isn't one of you S.O.B.s getting out of here alive.'
  There were about fifteen hundred farmers in the woods. The trucks
  didn't get twenty through. It was close in spirit to the American
  Revolution.

## c) 'Get Rich Quick' Schemes

While many people saw easy credit as a strength in the economy,
there were also considerable drawbacks. 'Get rich quick' was the aim
of many Americans in the 1920s; they invested in hugely speculative
ventures and inevitably many lost their money. Moreover, this situation provided golden opportunities for confidence tricksters and
crooks. In the early 1920s, for example, Charles Ponzi, a former veg-
etable seller conned thousands of gullible people into investing in his
ventures. He promised a 50 per cent profit within 90 days. Few, of
course, ever saw a cent of their money again. When sentencing him to
prison, the judge criticised his victims for their greed. Ponzi had not
forced anyone to part with their money.

The period saw other more large-scale speculations, notably during the Florida Land Boom and on the Stock Exchange in the latter part of the decade.

## i) The Florida Land Boom

While on bail awaiting trial, Ponzi found employment selling land in Florida. This was a venture well suited to his talents. Until this time, Florida was a relatively undeveloped state with a small population. In 1910, Miami was by far the biggest city with a population of 54,000. Then wealthy industrialists such as Henry M. Flagler of Standard Oil built elegant hotels in the state. With the coming of the motor car, its all-year-round sunshine became accessible to the middle classes and massive interest grew in the state as a paradise for vacations and retirement.

This led to a land boom. Between 1920 and 1925 the population of the state increased from 968,000 to 1.2 million. There were large-scale coastal developments. Inevitably parcels of land began to be sold to wealthy northerners on the basis of glossy brochures and salesmen's patter. People began to invest their money in unseen developments hoping to sell and make a quick profit. Often they paid on credit, with a 10 per cent deposit known as a 'binder'. Success stories abounded to fuel the boom. It was said that someone who had bought a parcel of land for $25 in 1900 had sold it for $150,000 25 years later.

However, the land boom could be sustained only by there being more buyers than sellers. But demand tailed off in 1926. There were scandals of land advertised as within easy access of the sea being, in fact, many miles inland or in the middle of swamps. One company, Manhattan Estates, advertised land as being three-quarters of a mile from the 'prosperous and fast growing' town of Nettie, a place that did not exist. Then nature played its part, with hurricanes in 1926 killing 400 people and leaving 50,000 homeless. With thousands of people bankrupted, the Florida land boom collapsed, leaving a coastline strewn with half-finished and storm-battered developments.

## ii) Stock Market Speculation

It seemed that few people were prepared to learn the lessons of Florida. As one way to get rich quickly closed so another seemed to open up. In the period 1927 to 1929 many Americans went 'Wall Street Crazy'. Easy credit meant many were able to invest in stocks and shares. They could be bought 'on the margin', on credit with loans from their broker. Increasingly, people purchased them not to invest in a company but as a speculation. If the price rose they would sell, making a quick and easy profit. For a time this seemed to work. Share prices seemed constantly to rise, some spectacularly so. According to the Wall Street Index, stock in the Radio Corporation of America rose from 85 to 420 in the course of 1928. There were stories of ordinary people making immense profits. Of course, in reality relatively few ordinary people ever dealt in shares; the figure was probably never higher than 1.5 million. What was more significant was that large concerns were investing their profits in the stock of others. For example, Bethlehem Steel Corporation and Electric Bond and Share each had invested $157 million in the market by late 1929. If prices should fall, these firms might lose their investments and have to reduce their own operations.

### iii) Banking System

The banking system of the USA was outmoded by the 1920s, although the central banking system dated only from 1913. Twelve regulatory reserve banks were headed by the Federal Reserve Board – usually known as 'the Fed' – with seven members appointed by the President. The system, it was felt, allowed banks to regulate themselves without the government having to interfere. However, there was a significant potential problem. The Reserve Banks represented the interests of the bankers and might not actually operate in the best interests of the nation if these clashed with what they perceived as being best for them.

While national banks had to join the centralised system, state banks did not. Most ordinary people's money, particularly in rural and semi-rural areas, was invested in the latter. In the 1920s there were almost 30,000 banks in the USA. Most were very small and therefore unable to withstand major setbacks. If they collapsed their depositors would probably lose virtually all their savings.

The Federal Reserve Board wanted to keep the market buoyant so it favoured low interest rates. This fuelled the easy credit discussed above. It also wanted to see a flow of gold from the USA to Europe so Europeans could afford to pay back their debts.

## d) Cycle of International Debt

This was at the heart of the economic problems of the USA. America's priority was for Europeans to repay the loans they had taken out to finance the First World War. When the problem of European countries' ability to repay came up, Coolidge is reported to have said, 'They hired the money, didn't they?' Although the quotation is possibly fictitious, it did accurately express the sentiment of many Americans. However, the simple truth was that Europeans just could not afford to repay the loans. The prohibitive tariffs made matters worse. European countries could not export their manufactured goods to the USA in great quantities; therefore they found it impossible to earn the money to repay the loans. Germany had, by the terms of the Treaty of Versailles, been forced to pay reparations to the victorious nations of Europe. The USA lent it the money to do so. With this money, the European victors repaid the USA what they could of the loans. The USA was then paying itself its money back. This situation became even more confused through the Dawes and Young Plans which scaled down German reparations. With Germany paying the European victors less, this meant that they in turn could repay less of their American loans. All in all, no one gained from an incredibly complex situation which, according to one commentator, would have made more sense if 'the US had taken the money out of one Treasury building and put it in another'.

The banks hoped the movement of gold to Europe would facilitate the victors' ability to repay the loans. American investors did increasingly invest in Europe, but this investment took place particularly in Germany where $3,900 million was invested after the Dawes Plan of April 1924. Wall Street brokers earned fat commissions for putting investors in touch with investees. Massive over-investment took place. Once again it was often a case of people hoping to make a quick profit without going too carefully into the actual details of the transaction. As a result, there were absurd examples such as the Bavarian village that asked for $125,000 to build a swimming pool, and received $3 million. However, with reparations scaled down, investment in Germany hardly helped the European victors repay their American loans. Its main effect was to make even more complex the tangle of international debt.

## e) Was the Boom Slowing Down?

The Boom was dependent on continuing domestic consumption. High tariffs and generally depressed economies in Europe meant that American producers could sell comparatively little abroad. There were, by the late 1920s, three indicators that the Boom was slowing down.

### i) Problems in Small Businesses

The decade, as we have seen, witnessed the growth of huge corporations with considerable marketing power. As a result, smaller businesses often faced hard times. During the course of the 1920s, for every four businesses that succeeded, three failed. The number of motor vehicle companies for example fell from 108 in 1920 to 44 by the end of the decade. The government was no more prepared to help out failing industrial concerns than it was the farmers.

### ii) The Construction Industry

Economic historians tend to agree that the state of the construction industry is generally a good indicator of the overall health of the economy. The mid 1920s saw a great boom in construction, particularly in housing, office building and highways. However, after 1926 demand began to tail off. This led to a fall in demand for building materials, skills such as plumbing, and building materials transportation. This, in turn, led to higher unemployment in construction-related businesses and had inevitable knock-on effects on concerns dependent on their custom.

### iii) Falling Domestic Demand

It is commonly agreed among historians that, by the late 1920s, production was outstripping demand. The domestic market was becoming flooded with goods that could not be sold. More and more people were in no position to spend on non-essential items. In April 1929, for example, it was estimated that 10 per cent of Philadelphia's labour force was unemployed even though the national unemployment statistics remained low. Irving Fisher, a Yale economist, estimated that in 1929, as many as 80 per cent of the American people were living close to subsistence – even when they were in work.

Workers could not on the whole look to trade unions for help. The government did nothing to protect them, and indeed the Supreme Court had blocked attempts to ban child labour and impose a minimum wage for women as being unconstitutional. Many employers operated 'yellow dog' clauses by which their employees were not allowed to join a union. During the 1920s union membership declined overall by one million. Interestingly, it tended to be employers in the new industries who were most anti-union, and during this period unions failed to get more than a toehold in these, while the older industries tended, as we have seen, to be in trouble during the decade. The government successfully sought injunctions against union activities earlier in the 1920s and by their close, employees generally were more anxious to keep their jobs than embark on union agitation.

With growth in the new industries beginning to slow, full-time employment fell and the economy entered into a downward spiral. A fall in income led to a fall in demand, which in turn led to a fall in production that added to unemployment and underemployment (short-time working). However, the fact that the economy had seemingly entered a downward spin was concealed by outward optimism and the frenzy of stock market speculation. It would largely be up to historians to untangle these threads to see with hindsight that a collapse had been inevitable.

## 5 The Strength of the Economy

> **KEY ISSUE** How real and widespread was the prosperity of the 1920s?

It is easy with hindsight to see the problems in the American economy. At the time, however, detailed understanding of how a developed economy works was far less sophisticated than it is today. While there was concern among experts and some even forecast accurately the coming collapse, they were largely voices in the wilderness. Many historians would agree with Hugh Brogan who wrote in 1985 that, 'At every stage the story displays the devastating consequences of a bland unawareness of economic and political essentials'.[3] Arthur Schlesinger Junior and J.K. Galbraith are influential historians who have been particularly scathing about the role of the government. Others, however, particularly economic historians, have been less critical, especially when comparing the American economy to others, notably those in Europe. After all, the figures denoting growth seem to speak for themselves. It is also important to note that the capitalist system survived the coming collapse almost intact. Many of the manufacturing and marketing companies of the 1920s have continued to operate to the present day, as have the banking and investment houses.

In a speech delivered at the end of the 1928 presidential election campaign, the victor, Herbert Hoover said:

1 We have ... in the 1920s ... decreased fear of poverty, fear of unemployment, the fear of old age. ...Prosperity is no idle expression. It is a job for every worker, it is the safety and safeguard of every business and every home. ... We are nearer today to the ideal of the abolition of
5 poverty and fear from the lives of men and women than ever before in any land.

While many Americans shared his confidence and optimism for the future, within a year the USA was in the grip of the deepest depression in its history.

## References

1  Snowman, *USA The Twenties to Vietnam* (B.T. Batsford; 1968), p. 20.
2  See L. Dumenil, 'Shifting perspectives on the 1920s', in (ed) J.E. Haynes, *Calvin Coolidge and the Coolidge Era* (Library of Congress, 1998), p. 76.
3  H. Brogan *The Penguin History of the United States of America* (Penguin 1990 edition), p. 532.

## Summary diagram
Prosperity?

| Year | 1922 | 1923 | 1924 | 1925 | 1926 | 1927 | 1928 |
|---|---|---|---|---|---|---|---|
| Political | Fordney–McCumber Act | Dawes Plan | McNary–Haugen bill. Tax cuts. | | Tax cuts | | Coolidge retired |
| Social/ economic | | | | Florida land boom. | Collapse of Florida land boom. Peak of construction boom. | Speculation on Stock Exchange. Ford closure until introduction of model 'A'. | |

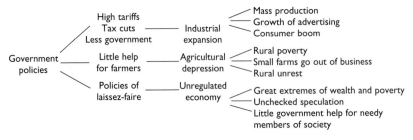

Government policies
- High tariffs
- Tax cuts ——— Industrial expansion
- Less government
  - Mass production
  - Growth of advertising
  - Consumer boom
- Little help for farmers ———— Agricultural depression
  - Rural poverty
  - Small farms go out of business
  - Rural unrest
- Policies of laissez-faire ————Unregulated economy
  - Great extremes of wealth and poverty
  - Unchecked speculation
  - Little government help for needy members of society

## Working on Chapter 3

This chapter attempts to do three things:

1) to consider what kind of president Calvin Coolidge was (section1).
2) to survey and account for the apparent prosperity in the USA in the 1920s (sections 2 and 3), and
3) to consider how real this prosperity actually was (sections 4 and 5).

In making notes you should focus on the following issues:
What was President Coolidge's attitude to government?
What evidence is there of a boom period?
What were the reasons for apparent prosperity?
What were the problems with the economy?

In order to consider more deeply the issue of how strong the American economy was during this period, you might find it helpful to construct a chart:

| Strengths | Weaknesses | Both strengths and weaknesses | Unsure |
|---|---|---|---|
| | | | |

The columns should include factors you consider appropriate to each. When you have completed the chart, you can expand your notes by explaining why you have placed the factors where you have done. You should then be able to make an informed judgement on the strength of the American economy in the 1920s.

## Answering essay questions on Chapter 3

Many economic questions look at the 1920s in the context of the Wall Street Crash and these will be considered at the end of Chapter 3. Questions specifically on the 1920s may be straightforward:

**1.** What were the reasons for the prosperity in the USA in the 1920s?

However, they often invite you to discuss how far all economic sectors and regions shared in the prosperity:

**2.** How widespread in the USA was the prosperity of the 1920s?

Here you need to consider different economic areas such as farming and manufacturing, and different regions, particularly in terms of the rural/urban divide before coming to an informed judgement in your conclusion.

## Source-based questions on Chapter 3

### 1. Advertising

Read carefully the two extracts from car brochures (page 34). Answer the following questions:

**a)** Advertisers talk of a 'unique selling point' with which to market a product. What is the 'unique selling point' in each of these extracts? *(5 marks)*
**b)** What factors are mentioned in common? Explain why this should be so. *(5 marks)*
**c)** What are the strengths and weaknesses of these advertisements as historical evidence? *(5 marks)*

### 2. Business

Read carefully the Businessman's Prayer (page 32) and the extract from The Man Nobody Knew (page 34). Answer the following questions:

**a)** Explain in your own words the argument in the extract from The Man Nobody Knew. How effective do you find it? Explain your answer carefully. *(4 marks)*

**b)** What is the value of these two sources to an historian studying American business in the 1920s? *(8 marks)*

**c)** Using both sources and your own knowledge, how accurately do you think the sources illustrate American attitudes to business in the 1920s? *(8 marks)*

## 3. *Farming*

Read Calvin Coolidge's reasons for vetoing the McNary–Haugen bill (page 40) and Emil Loriks' account (page 40). Answer the following questions:

**a)** In Loriks' account, what is meant by 'sales'? *(2 marks)*

**b)** Explain in your own words why Coolidge opposed the McNary–Haugen bill. How persuasive do you find his arguments? *(5 marks)*

**c)** Whose side is Lorkis on? Support your answer with evidence from the extract. *(5 marks)*

**d)** What does Lorkis mean by the phrase: 'It was close in spirit to the American Revolution' (lines 18–19)? *(3 marks)*

## 4. *Government Attitudes*

Read Coolidge's message to Congress (page 26) and Hoover's speech in 1928 (page 45). Study the photograph of rural poverty (page 38). Answer the following questions:

**a)** In what ways do the two speeches agree? *(3 marks)*

**b)** Coolidge says people should be optimistic. What evidence does Hoover offer to support this view? *(4 marks)*

**c)** How does the photograph differ from the two accounts of American prosperity? *(4 marks)*

**d)** Using evidence known to you, which groups would **i)** support, and **ii)** oppose the views presented in the two speeches? Explain your answer carefully. *(9 marks)*

# 4 The Collapse of the Stock Market

## POINTS TO CONSIDER

Why did the US Stock Market collapse in October 1929?

**KEY DATE**

**1929 Oct** 'Wall Street Crash' – collapse of the Stock Market

## 1 Introduction

In October 1929 the New York Stock Exchange, handling about 61 per cent of stock transactions in the USA, crashed. Crashes in other stock exchanges throughout the country soon followed. While the collapse in Wall Street was not unexpected among many financial experts, their warnings had gone largely unheeded. The event triggered shock and trauma among many, including those seemingly unaffected financially by the collapse. The Wall Street Crash is perhaps the most famous historic event in the period covered by this book; and it is the purpose of this chapter first to describe what actually happened and then to examine its causes and significance.

## 2 The Wall Street Crash

> **KEY ISSUE** How the Wall Street Crash came about.

On Thursday 24 October 1929 a massive amount of selling began in the New York Stock Exchange, forcing prices down. This led to more selling still as brokers feared they would be left with worthless stock. By 11 am a mad panic had set in. US Steel, which had opened that morning at 205.5, was down to 193.5, General Electric had fallen from 315 to 283 and Radio had collapsed from 68.75 to 44.5. No one seemingly could understand what was going on. People are afraid of the unknown, of things they cannot control – and what was going on here was certainly out of control. On one wall of the Stock Exchange was a large board recording transactions; this was called the ticker. Unfortunately as the volume of sales mushroomed, it could no longer keep pace and began to fall badly behind. At ten-minute intervals, a separate bond ticker in the corner would punch out a list of selected up-to-date prices. As brokers hushed to hear these read out, they realised with horror that stocks bought possibly just moments earlier were now worth considerably less than they had agreed to pay for them. As more and more brokers rushed to sell, the scenes became so wild that the police had to be called in to restore order. As news of the panic spread, an excited crowd gathered outside the building. It was even said that some coach tour companies diverted their vehicles to take New York sightseers to witness the goings-on. A workman repairing a high building was believed to be a broker contemplating suicide. He was possibly inadvertently responsible for the myth that bankrupted brokers were throwing themselves from the rooftops. Comparatively few brokers did, in fact, go bankrupt. It was largely their clients' wealth that was being lost.

Frederick Lewis Allen painted a vivid picture of the tension that day:

1   As the price structure crumbled there was a sudden stampede to get
    out from under. By eleven o'clock traders on the floor of the Stock
    Exchange were in a wild scramble to 'sell at the market'. Long before
    the lagging ticker could tell what was happening, word had gone out by
5   telephone and telegraph that the bottom was dropping out of things
    and the selling orders redoubled in volume. The leading stocks were
    going down between sales. Down, down, down. ... Where were the
    bargain hunters who were supposed to come to the rescue at times like
    these? Where were the investment trusts, which were expected to
10  provide a cushion for the market by making new purchases at low
    prices? Where were the big operators who had declared that they were
    still bullish? Where were the powerful bankers who were supposed to
    be able at any moment to support prices? There seemed to be no support
    whatsoever. Down, down, down. The roar of voices which rose
15  from the floor of the Exchange had become a roar of panic.

A meeting of six eminent bankers was going on in the offices of J.P. Morgan Ltd at 23 Wall Street. There, each agreed to put up $40 million to shore up the market. Thomas W. Lamont, senior partner at J.P. Morgan Ltd, held a press conference. 'There has been a little distress on the Stock Market,' he said, with a masterly sense of understatement. He went on to explain that this was due entirely to a technical difficulty, and the situation was 'susceptible to betterment'. Meanwhile, the vice-president of the Stock Exchange, Richard Whitney, a floor broker for J.P. Morgan Ltd, was buying stock above current prices in lots of 10,000. The bankers having come to the rescue, confidence returned and the situation did become better. At the close of the day the New York Times Index, based on an aggregate of 25 leading industrial stocks, was only 12 points down. The ticker however did not record the final transactions until eight minutes past seven in the evening – business closed at 3 pm – and clerks worked long into the night on the accounts. One clerk reported that, 'We had to stay up all night figuring. We'd work till one o'clock and go to the LaSalle Hotel and get up about five and get some breakfast and continue figuring margin accounts'. Altogether, nearly 13 million shares had changed hands. By comparison, a normal day's transactions would be about 3 million. Stock Market employees, letting off steam after such a frenzied day, caused the police to be called to Wall Street again.

For the next few days calm was restored in the market. Everyone who had weathered the storm breathed a sigh of relief. Writing about the market on Friday 25 October, the New York Times reported, 'Secure in the knowledge that the most powerful banks in the country stood ready to prevent a recurrence, the financial community relaxed its anxiety yesterday'. A Boston investment trust placed an advertisement in the Wall Street Journal: 'S-T-E-A-D-Y Everybody! Calm thinking is in order. Heed the words of America's greatest bankers'. On Sunday, churchgoers heard that a divine warning had been sent concerning the dangers of financial greed and speculation; but while acknowledging the warning, it was doubtful if it would be seriously heeded. Most newspapers were ostensibly confident that the Stock Market was healthy and the days ahead would see a rush to buy at the new lower prices.

In the event, however, while the volume of trading on Monday was less than that of the previous Thursday, the fall in prices was far more severe. The New York Times Index showed a drop of 49 points on the day's trading and no Richard Whitney had appeared with orders to buy. After the close of business, bankers held a two-hour meeting at J.P. Morgan Ltd. Those expecting them to come again to the rescue were to be sadly disappointed. It was not their business, it was explained, to protect stock market prices, but simply to ensure the market was orderly. Next day, confidence collapsed completely. This was Tuesday 29 October, the day of the Wall Street Crash. Altogether, 16,410,030 shares were sold and the New York Times Index fell a further 43 points. In the chaos of mad selling, there was talk of closing the Exchange at noon, but it was felt this would simply increase the panic. However, the Exchange did remain closed the next day, and only opened Thursday afternoon during the remainder of the week. Prices continued to fall, and despite occasional rallies, in the words of J.K. Galbraith, 'No feature of the Great Crash was more remarkable than the way it passed from climax to anti-climax to destroy again and again the hope that the worst had passed'. In a few weeks, it is alleged, as much as $30 billion had been lost. This represented a sum almost as great as that which the USA had spent on its involvement in the First World War.

The following table gives some indication of the level of losses:

| Company | Share price on 3.9.1929 | Share price on 13.11.1929 |
| --- | --- | --- |
| American Can | 187.86 | 86 |
| Ananconda Copper | 131.50 | 70 |
| General Motors | 72.75 | 36 |
| Montgomery Ward | 137.86 | 49.25 |
| Radio | 101 | 28 |
| Woolworth | 100.37 | 52.25 |
| Electric Share and Bond | 186.75 | 50.25 |

However, it is worth remembering that even after October 1929 prices still stood higher than they had done at any time during the previous year. What had been wiped out were the spectacular gains of the first nine months of 1929. Even after the Crash, experts failed to see the damage done. On 26 October, for example, the Harvard Economic Society felt that 'despite its severity, we believe that the slump in stock prices will prove an intermediate movement and not the precursor of a business depression such as would entail prolonged further liquidation'. Not until 1932, when it was clear that the Great Depression was going to continue into the long term and recovery was not, as President Hoover had continued to insist, just around the corner, did prices really plunge. On 8 June 1932, for example, the New York Times Index closed at 58.46.

It is often popularly believed that the Wall Street Crash led to the Great Depression. However, many historians have argued that it was simply one manifestation of a Depression already well on the way. Moreover, stock markets had crashed before and have done since without any ensuing economic depression. In order to analyse the part played in this history by the Wall Street Crash, it is necessary, first to identify its causes and then to examine its impact within the context of an economy whose growth was, as we have seen in Chapter 3, already slowing.

# 3 Causes of the Wall Street Crash

> **KEY ISSUE** What were the reasons behind the Stock Market collapse?

## a) The Nature of the Bull Market

The Stock Market contained the seeds of its own collapse. To understand these we need to examine how the market operated in the years up to the Wall Street Crash. A 'bullish' market is characterised by a large volume of buying and selling. Reference has already been made in Chapter 2 to the nature of the Stock Market between 1927 and 1929 which earned it the nickname 'Great Bull Market'. The New York Times Index averages (which reflected the volume of trading) rose from 106 to 181 between May 1924 and December 1925. They increased to 245 by December 1927, and by September 1929 the figure was 542. Brokers spoke excitedly of breaking the ceiling of five million transactions in one day, but on 23 November 1928, shortly after the electoral victory of President Hoover, seven million transactions took place. The cost of a seat on the New York Stock Exchange rose to $580,000. America, it seemed, went 'Wall Street Crazy'. There were scores of anecdotes to encourage further speculation, such as those about the nurse who became rich on the stock market tips of grateful patients and about the broker's valet who made $250,000. The amount of trading on the market grew, particularly after Hoover's victory when optimism in the boundlessness of American prosperity, fuelled by statements of confidence emanating from the government, seemed unshakeable. In summer 1929, for example, brokers' loans climbed towards the figure of $6 billion as compared to $3.5 billion at the end of 1927, with prices of popular stocks rising dramatically.

There are many causes of the bull market, not least, as we have seen, the desire of people to 'get rich quick'. However, historians agree that the trigger was the decision by the Federal Reserve Board to lower rediscount rates (the interest rate at which member banks borrowed from the reserve banks) in August 1927 from 4 per cent to 3.5 per cent. This step was actually taken to encourage American trade abroad but in fact the main effect of lower interest rates was to encourage borrowing at home. The financial community, it should be remembered, was very confident in the strength of the economy and those with surplus funds naturally wanted to use them to make even more money. The Stock Exchange offered just such an opportunity. Wall Street stockbroking firms encouraged people to invest in shares by opening more and more offices – in 1919 there were 500 but in October 1928 there were 1,192. An estimated 50,000 people bought their shares 'on the margin'. This meant they put down only a fraction of the price, borrowing the rest from the broker who in turn borrowed largely from the banks to pay for the shares. With prices rising constantly, few paused to consider what might happen if they fell, leaving them still having to pay for depreciated assets. Many people no doubt saw buying 'on the margin' in the same way as they saw hire-purchase arrangements – as a way of buying now and paying later – except by this method they could pay out of the profits their shares were expected to make. It seemed a foolproof way of growing rich. They were further encouraged by articles in the popular press. 'Everyone Ought to be Rich' for example appeared in the Ladies'

Home Journal. The author showed that if readers saved $15 per month and invested this in good common stock, if they then allowed dividends to accumulate, they would, at the end of 21 years, have at least $80,000; this would give them interest payments of $400 per month. How could anyone fail? Could investors even afford to miss out? They were advised to consider the wealth of someone today who had bought 100 shares in General Motors in 1919; they were warned that prices would never be as low as this again. With endorsements on the strength and soundness of the market from the President as well as from influential businessmen, people could even afford to overextend themselves – and many did.

J.K. Galbraith has identified three types of purchasers of shares:[1]

i) Those who believed in the strength of the enterprise in which they bought their shares. This group normally expected their dividends to come from the profits of the concern; often they would keep their shares for a considerable period of time, take an interest in the company, attend share-holders' meetings and the like. In a stable market, they would tend to be the biggest group of purchasers of shares.

However, this was not the case in the bull market of the late 1920s. Many people were buying shares in concerns not in the expectation that the concern might make a profit, but simply that the value of its stock would increase, giving them the opportunity to sell at a quick profit. Radio, for example, saw its share prices rise from 94.5 to 504 in 18 months without ever having paid a single dividend. This very fact alone helps demonstrate that it was a speculative market rather than one based on real economic growth. There was no indication that Radio was a reliable and prosperous company other than the demand for its shares. There was even a faddishness about share purchase. Buying stock in aeronautical companies became popular after the exploits of aviators such as Charles Lindburgh, the first man to fly solo across the Atlantic.

ii) Those who sought to get rich quick. They were, perhaps, the majority of players in the 'Great Bull Market'. They are sometimes described as the innocents who did not understand the workings of the market, although they thought they did. Generally, they expected prices to keep rising, with themselves selling at optimum times to maximise their profits. Characteristically, this group bought stock purely as speculation. They had no thought of investing in an actual concern but bought and sold simply on the expected movement of prices. Not unnaturally, this was the group that tended to lose heavily in the Wall Street Crash.

iii) Those who were 'streetwise' and took full advantage of the boom, intending to get out before the inevitable collapse. These tended to be the large-scale financiers and bankers. Typically, many of these attempted to inflate prices artificially. William Durant, for example, operated the famous 'bull pool'; he and his colleagues bought and sold shares back and forth to each other, giving the impression of great market interest in a particular issue. Once unwary outsiders began to buy, sending the prices still higher, they would sell, making a huge profit and as the prices then fell, the outsiders would be left with much depreciated stock. There was little regulation of activities such as 'insider dealing' and it was easy to take advantage of others' naivety.

In fact, the market was not characterised by an unbroken rise in prices. There were falls – in March, June and December 1928, and in March 1929 for example. However, the market always recovered, casting doubts on those financial experts who warned that prices were dangerously high. As early as 5 January 1928, Moody's Investment Service warned that stocks had 'overdiscounted anticipated progress' and wondered 'how much a readjustment may be required to place the stock market in a sound position'. Roger Babson seems to have been remarkably farsighted when, in September 1929, he warned that existing prosperity rested precariously on a 'state of mind' and not on economic facts. He went on to predict a crash that would lead to massive unemployment and economic depression. However, these and others were criticised as being overpessimistic, threatening to undermine the economic well-being of the nation. Both President Coolidge and President Hoover had given periodic reassuring noises, although the former had been alerted as early as 1927 by William R. Zipley of Harvard to the fact that there were serious problems with the Stock Exchange. Coolidge did not believe it was the job of Goverment to involve itself in the Stock Market. Hoover tried to blame Governor Roosevelt of New York for the Crash, saying it was his responsibility, which he had failed to exercise, to regulate Wall Street. At the time, few listened any attempt to shift the blame by Hoover. However, Roosevelt had not shown any public concern about the volume of stock exchange trading and others said that the Governor of New York should have done more.

The truth was that most experts seemed confident that the market was strong and the vast majority of people had little reason to doubt them. For example, on 17 October 1929 Professor Irving Fisher stated that prices had reached 'what looks to be a permanently high plateau'. The fact that we can see with hindsight that the market was in reality so unstable that its eventual collapse was inevitable should not blind us to this optimism and faith in the strength of the market. It is worth remembering too that experts at the time often had a nineteenth-century understanding of the way markets worked and had failed to see how these had become outmoded by twentieth-century developments such as the expansion of credit.

## b) The Banking System

One of the most frequent criticisms of the Great Bull Market was that there was no effective control over its activities. The government, as we have seen, pursued policies of laissez-faire that tended to favour big business, and the powers of the central banking system were severely limited. The Federal Reserve Board could intervene in the market in three principal ways:

i) Authorise the sale of government securities on the market, hoping purchasers might prefer these safe investments to those which paid higher dividends but were riskier. In the event, instead of doing this, the Board actually purchased government securities from the banks, which meant, of course, the banks now had more funds to lend for possibly risky investments. While the Board did this for sound reasons – economic growth was slowing – its major effect was to stimulate borrowing and Stock Market speculation.

ii) Raise the rediscount rate to discourage further borrowing. As we have seen, the Federal Reserve Board unwittingly helped spark off the bull market by reducing the rediscount rate from 4 per cent to 3.5 per cent in spring 1927. Concerned at the vast spread of credit, it did finally raise the rediscount rate to 5 per cent in December 1928, but this had little effect on a market running rampant. The Board indeed overruled a proposal by the New York Reserve Bank to raise the rediscount rate further to 6 per cent. A rise at this level would in any event have been quite inadequate to deter borrowing at a time when brokers' loans were finding plenty of takers at twice that level of interest. To make matters worse, non-banking concerns such as Bethlehem Steel and Chrysler were also lending to brokers.

In this situation, the Federal Reserve Board seemed quite powerless. It did raise the rediscount rate to 6 per cent in August 1929 but, as expected, this had no noticeable effect on checking speculation. The Board was worried conversely that if the rediscount rate was increased too much, a crash might be precipitated. Many senior bankers did probably privately realise just how delicate the market actually was and were very wary of meddling too much with it lest they might set off a panic and possible collapse.

Moreover, the bankers who made up the Federal Reserve system had what they considered to be sound reasons for not raising interest rates. Firstly, because they were bankers, they tended to put their banking interests before those of the national interest. They had no wish to hurt banks (and themselves) by making them pay more for funds by raising interest rates. Secondly, it should be remembered that a prime banking consideration was the promotion of foreign trade; higher interest rates may have made American goods too expensive for foreign buyers in already depressed foreign markets. The simple fact was that, while it may well have been in the interests of the country to control credit through higher interest rates, the picture was much more complex than that and other considerations dictated that higher interest rates would not be a satisfactory option. The Stock Market meanwhile continued to operate unchecked.

iii) The Federal Reserve Board could offer moral leadership. On 2 February 1929, for example, it issued the following statement:

1  The Federal Reserve Act does not in the opinion of the Federal Reserve Board contemplate the use of the resources of the Federal Reserve Banks for the creation or extension of speculative credit. A member bank is not within its reasonable claims for rediscount facilities at its
5  Federal Reserve Bank when it borrows either for the purpose of making speculative loans or for the purpose of maintaining speculative loans.

The immediate result of this statement was a fall in stock prices and an increase in the interest rate on brokers' loans to as high as 20 per cent. The secretive meetings of the Federal Reserve Board certainly unnerved the market, again demonstrating how delicate its equipoise actually was. In the event, in what has been called 'the single most irresponsible decision of 1929', Charles A. Mitchell, President of New York's National City Bank and a director of the New York Federal Reserve Bank, announced on 26 March that if money became tight as a result of higher rediscount rates, his bank would pump a further $25 million into the brokers' loan market:

> We feel that we have an obligation which is paramount to any Federal Reserve warning or anything else to avert any dangerous crisis in the money market.

Mitchell was attacked in Congress for sabotaging the policy of the Federal Reserve Board. The accusation was certainly true. The market recovered and prices soared until the crash. The Federal Reserve Board was shown to have been an irrelevance to the market, its powers wholly inadequate to supervise what was going on. However, it is also true that the Board could have asked Congress for more powers, for example over the control of credit, but it did not. Anyway, it is unlikely that they would have been granted had they been requested. There are five possible reasons for this:

i) The mood of the country was generally against regulation in any aspect of economic life.

ii) The Federal Reserve system was made up of bankers who operated principally in the interests of their own banks and, if these clashed with the national interest, the former almost always prevailed.

iii) The bull market was associated in the public eye with prosperity. It had not collapsed. To the average layman, it seemed to be in a very healthy state, and there would have been no great support for its regulation.

iv) The main policy of the Federal Reserve System was to encourage the movement of gold to Europe through increased trade. This necessitated low interest rates. One of the leading American bankers of this period was Benjamin Strong, Governor of the New York Federal Reserve Bank. This policy was particularly associated with him. Strong died in 1928. Some historians have argued that had he lived he would have had the skills and influence to curb speculation without risking a market crash. However, although Strong was privately concerned about the level of speculation and borrowing, there is no evidence to suggest that he would have done anything more than anyone else to stop it. Raising the rediscount rate would have put the USA's prevailing trading policies in jeopardy.

## c) Loss of Confidence

It has been emphasised that the market structure was maintained largely by the confidence people had in it. Historians point to various reasons why that confidence collapsed in October 1929, rather than at any other time:

i) The British financial empire built up by Clarence Hatry collapsed at this time. This showed that enterprises financed by debt, as his was, were vulnerable, and investors in the USA looked askance at some of the concerns in which they had stock.

ii) Rumours spread that many of the biggest players on the Stock Market such as Bernard Baruch and Joseph Kennedy were selling. Perhaps they knew something that mere mortals did not!

iii) There were rumours that the Federal Reserve Board was about to tighten credit facilities.

iv) In this increasing atmosphere of uncertainty, lenders began to call in credit. For example, over the weekend between 25 and 28 October 1929 banks began to demand repayment from the brokers to whom they had lent money. The brokers in turn began to put the squeeze on their clients, who had to sell in order to repay their loans. This exacerbated the cycle of selling. Pressure for repayment meant that credit was evaporating. One lady, presented by her broker with a bill for $100,000 demanded, 'How could I lose $100,000. I never had $100,000'. While this anecdote may well be of doubtful veracity, it is nevertheless a good illustration of the naivety of many Stock Market gamblers. They really had little idea of what they were doing in buying and selling shares, and either did not realise or chose to ignore the fact that prices could indeed collapse as well as soar. In the event, it tended to be the 'innocents' who were ruined by the Wall Street Crash – although this is not to suggest that other, more professional financial interests did not also suffer.

However, the truth is that the market, supported by so little real wealth, could have collapsed at any time. There is little really noteworthy about the actual timing. Here are two differing accounts of the causes of the Crash by those who lived through it:

> People were speculating. Now who are you gonna blame aside from themselves? It's their fault. See my point? If you gamble and make a mistake, why pick on somebody else? It's your fault, don't you see? ...
> Way back in the '29s, People were wearing 20 dollar silk shirts and

5 throwing their money around like crazy. If they had been buying the $2
Arrow shirts and putting the other eighteen in the bank, they wouldn't
have been in the condition they were in. In 1929, I had a friend who
speculated. He'd say 'What's good?' I'd say, 'We're selling high-grade
first mortgage bonds on Commonwealth Edison.' 'Oh, hell', he'd say,
10 'five per cent. I make ten percent on the Stock Market.' He was buying
on the margin. He thought he was rich. Know what happened to him?
He blew his brains out. The Government had nothing to do with that.
It's people.

*Martin DeVries*

1 The Crash – it didn't happen in one day. There were a great many
warnings. The country was crazy. Everybody was in the Stock Market
whether he could afford it or not. ... A great many holding company pyramids were unsound, really fictitious values. Mr Insull was a case in
5 point. It was a mad dream of get-rich-quick.
It wasn't only brokers involved in margin accounts. It was banks. They
had a lot of stinking banks. The banks worked in as casual a way as the
brokers did.
You had no governmental control of margins, so people could buy on a
10 shoestring. And when they began pulling the plug you had a deluge of
weakness. You also had short selling and a lack of rules. There were
many cases of staid, reputable bankers making securities available on
special deals – below the market price – for their friends. Anything
went, and anything did go.

*John Hersch*

Having studied the above analysis and read these accounts, what do
you think are the reasons the Stock Market collapsed as it did?

# 4 Effects of the Wall Street Crash

> **KEY ISSUE** What were the economic and social effects of the Wall
> Street Crash?

## a) Did the Wall Street Crash Cause the Great Depression?

Although the myth is persuasive, the Crash did not actually cause the
Depression. This was widely recognised at the time and has been
largely accepted by historians ever since. American business was too
big and too diversified to be influenced to a decisive extent by the
Stock Market. There is little doubt that by the time of the Crash, the
Depression was well on the way for the reasons discussed in Chapter
3. As well as overspeculation, living on credit, and get-rich-quick
schemes, there were the great inequalities of wealth and prosperity;
problems with international trade; depression in staple industries
such as agriculture; overproduction and falling domestic demand

which had already resulted in serious problems in the building and, to a certain extent, in the car industries. There is little doubt that the Crash was more of an effect than a cause of the Depression, although we have to recognise that effects can exacerbate the problems they have resulted from, and the importance of the Crash should not be minimised. It was an important trigger, as we shall see, in worsening the Depression. Certainly too, the nature of the bull market added to the frailty of the economy.

## b) Effects of the Crash on the Economy

There is some disagreement on the relative significance of the effects, although most commentators are in broad agreement about what they actually were.

i) Individuals and business concerns lost billions. Thousands were bankrupted and even those who remained solvent were often hard hit. Clarence Mitchell's bank lost half its assets; the President of Union Cigar plunged to his death from the ledge of a New York Hotel when stock in his company fell from $113.50 to $4 in a single day. Even the Rockerfellers lost over $50 million in a vain effort to shore up the market.

The point is, of course, that people who lost heavily could no longer afford to consume or invest further. So much of the prosperity of the 1920s had been based on continuing demand for consumer durables. Goods which do not have to be regularly replaced, such as motor cars and electrical appliances, tend not to be replaced when times are hard. Therefore, the industries that supplied them in the USA at this time found demand slipping further. The power of advertising, for example, had little influence on a people who increasingly had nothing to spend. All this was eventually to lead to a massive level of company cutbacks and often bankruptcy. As workforces were laid off, there was still less money within the economy for spending and this led in turn to a further slowing as the economy wound its inexorable way into a generally depressed condition.

ii) The Stock Market Crash led to the collapse of credit. Loans were called in and new ones refused. Although stock might now have no value, it was nevertheless accepted by banks from brokers who couldn't otherwise repay their debts. With their own assets thereby reduced, banks were even less likely to make further loans. This, of course, led to a credit squeeze and to a concomitant fall in demand and business activity. No one, it seemed, was prepared to take a financial risk.

## c) Effects of the Crash on the Culture of Society

The Crash signified an end of confidence. To so many people, Wall Street had symbolised the prosperity of the 1920s. The Stock Market had seemed invulnerable. J.K. Galbraith has argued that even though the number of Stock Market players was comparatively few, the idea of Stock Market speculation had become central to the culture of society.[2] In other words, it had become almost a certainty, like a belief in the ideas behind the Declaration of Independence or even the pioneer spirit that had 'won the west'. It was an integral part of what it meant to be 'American'. The warning voices had been ignored. People had chosen to listen instead to the soothing tones coming from the White House and big business. When those same soothing voices continued in the wake of the Crash, they were no longer believed. Their credibility was shot – but more, they were almost despised as belonging to those who had let the nation down, had destroyed its fundamental beliefs. In this situation, national confidence sank to rock bottom. This is in turn fuelled the Depression to whose onset people had for too long been oblivious.

In the words of Frederick Allen:

1   … Prosperity is more than an economic condition; it is a state of mind. The Big Bull Market had been more than the climax of a business cycle; it had been the climax of a cycle in American mass thinking and mass emotion.

5   There was hardly a man or a woman whose attitude toward life had not been affected by it in some degree and was not now affected by the sudden and brutal shattering of hope. With the Big Bull Market gone and prosperity going, Americans were soon to find themselves living in an altered world which called for new adjustments, new ideas, new

10   habits of thought and a new order of values. The psychological climate was changing; the ever shifting currents of American life were turning into new channels.

With the country increasingly in the grip of the Depression, with confidence shattered and new uncertainties pervading society, attention now began to focus on the incumbent in the White House, Herbert Hoover.

## References

1   J.K. Galbraith, 'The Wall Street Crash', in Purnell, *History of the Twentieth Century*, vol 3, pp. 1249–1252.
2   *Ibid.*

**Summary diagram**
The Collapse of the Stock Market

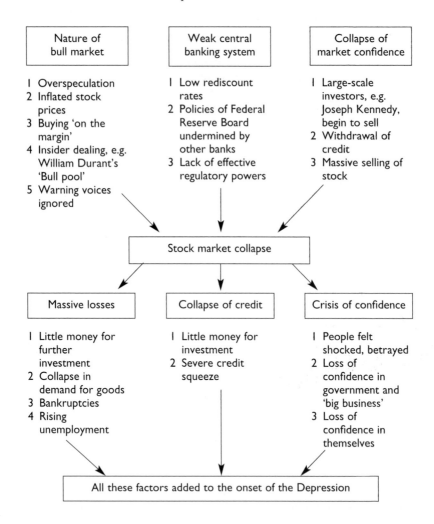

| Nature of bull market | Weak central banking system | Collapse of market confidence |
|---|---|---|
| 1 Overspeculation<br>2 Inflated stock prices<br>3 Buying 'on the margin'<br>4 Insider dealing, e.g. William Durant's 'Bull pool'<br>5 Warning voices ignored | 1 Low rediscount rates<br>2 Policies of Federal Reserve Board undermined by other banks<br>3 Lack of effective regulatory powers | 1 Large-scale investors, e.g. Joseph Kennedy, begin to sell<br>2 Withdrawal of credit<br>3 Massive selling of stock |

Stock market collapse

| Massive losses | Collapse of credit | Crisis of confidence |
|---|---|---|
| 1 Little money for further investment<br>2 Collapse in demand for goods<br>3 Bankruptcies<br>4 Rising unemployment | 1 Little money for investment<br>2 Severe credit squeeze | 1 People felt shocked, betrayed<br>2 Loss of confidence in government and 'big business'<br>3 Loss of confidence in themselves |

All these factors added to the onset of the Depression

## Working on Chapter 4

This chapter has three aims in terms of content:

**i)** to give an account of the Wall Street Crash (section 2).
**ii)** to examine the causes of the Crash (section 3).
**iii)** to consider its effects, particularly in relation to the onset of the Great Depression (section 4).

Your notes should focus on these issues.

The chapter is laid out to demonstrate the difference between description and analysis. The second section on the Wall Street Crash itself is mainly descriptive and the latter two are based on analysis. Put simply, description tells you what happened; analysis looks more deeply behind what happened by asking such questions as 'Why did it happen?', 'How did it happen?', and 'What were the implications of it happening?'. In your work you should normally be aiming for analysis but it is, of course, difficult to analyse an event you know little about. It is necessary to get the facts first. Description involves a lower level set of skills than analysis but you have to go through them in order to proceed.

Therefore, you should first make notes about what happened.

Moving on to the causes of the Crash, you may need to consider why people placed such faith in the Bull Market. To help you with this you may need to go back to Chapter 3 sections 3 d) (page 35) and 4c) (pages 40–42). It will also help if you complete the following chart:

| Strengths of the Bull Market | Weaknesses of the Bull Market |
|---|---|
|  |  |

When making notes on the banking system, consider in particular how Mitchell undermined the Board's policy and the messages this sent out to Stock Market brokers and investors. You could also complete the following chart:

| How the banking system could influence the market | What it actually did |
|---|---|
|  |  |

Your notes on the effects of the Wall Street Crash could focus on how far the Crash caused the Depression and how far it simply made worse a Depression that was already on its way.

In this section you need to realise that it is always difficult to deal with intangibles; the information in this section cannot be measured in the way that economic data can. In writing it, I have relied on literary rather than quantitative evidence. Much of it will inevitably be subjective.

## Answering essay questions on Chapter 4

The Wall Street Crash features commonly in examination questions, which are usually related to cause and effect. Standard questions include those that are seemingly straightforward:

**1.** Account for the Wall Street Crash.

It is important that you understand what is required by this question. It asks you for an account of why it happened rather than for an account of what happened. Remember that very few marks are given in an essay for description. However, the best answers to the above will give more than just a list of possible causes and a description of each. They will do some or all of the following:

a) Look at the different types of causes. For example which were the triggers which set off the Crash and which were the underlying causes without which the Crash could not have happened but did not in themselves make it happen? One way to tackle this is first to brainstorm the causes and then go on to categorise them into triggers and underlying causes. Generally the short-term causes are the triggers. If the long-term causes made things happen in themselves, they would not be long-term causes!

b) Place the causes in order of relative importance. In order to consider the relative importance of different causes you need to look at the circumstances in which they operated. If the market had been regulated more effectively, for example, could there have been so much overspeculation? How important was the comparatively weak central banking system?

Both types of planning work particularly well if you first do them on your own and then compare your findings with those of a partner or within a small group. A little discussion can add a lot to collective understanding!

More probably in the second year of 'A' level, you may find questions such as:

**Was the Great Depression well under way before the collapse of the Stock Market in October 1929?**

As in the second essay listed above, this question would require knowledge of the economy in the 1920s particularly in terms of pointers to a coming collapse, e.g. poor farm prices, the rate of business collapse, 'Get Rich Quick' schemes and overproduction. This knowledge could be coupled with a section on the effects of the Crash so that a judgement could be made as to how far the Crash was a causal factor and how far an effect in itself of the Depression which hit the USA in 1929. Examiners are looking for a balanced and considered answer supported with relevant evidence.

## Source-based questions on Chapter 4

### 1. Thursday 24 October 1929
Read carefully the extract by Frederick Lewis Allen on page 50 and study the figures showing the collapse of share prices on page 52.

a) Explain carefully the following terms: **i)** 'the lagging ticker' (line 4), **ii)** 'the big operators who had declared that they were still bullish' (lines 11–12) *(4 marks)*
b) How does the writer of this extract convey the mounting sense of panic? Give evidence from the extract to explain your answer. *(6 marks)*
c) What are the advantages of statistical evidence such as given in this list over written evidence such as the extract by Frederick Lewis Allen? *(4 marks)*
d) What are the advantages of written evidence such as that given by Frederick Lewis Allen over statistical tables? *(4 marks)*
e) Why should historians use both kinds of evidence? *(2 marks)*

### 2. The Role of the Banks
Read carefully the two extracts concerning the role of the banks on page 57.

a) What five things can you learn about the role of the banks from these two extracts? *(5 marks)*
b) With reference to these extracts, explain how Charles A. Mitchell undermined the policy of the Federal Reserve Board. *(5 marks)*

### 3. Causes of the Wall Street Crash
Read carefully the accounts by Martin DeVries and John Hersch on pages 58–9.

a) Who does DeVries blame for the Wall Street Crash? *(3 marks)*
b) Does Hersch, on the basis of these extracts, agree with DeVries in his interpretation? Explain your answer carefully with reference to the texts. *(5 marks)*
c) Which of the two accounts do you find the most persuasive? Explain your answer. *(7 marks)*
d) These two accounts are both oral testimonies recorded many years after the time. What are the advantages and disadvantages of this type of evidence? *(10 marks)*

### 4. The Effects of the Wall Street Crash
Read carefully the extract by Frederick Lewis Allen on page 61.

a) What, according to Allen, was the significance of the Wall Street Crash? *(5 marks)*
b) What evidence does he give to support his views? *(5 marks)*
c) On the basis of your own knowledge, how far did the Wall Street Crash cause the Great Depression? *(10 marks)*

# 5 President Hoover and the Great Depression

## POINTS TO CONSIDER

This chapter attempts to do four things: i) to consider the background and beliefs of President Hoover; ii) to consider the nature and severity of the problems which he faced; iii) to consider how he responded to these problems; and iv) to consider why he was defeated by Franklin D. Roosevelt in the 1932 presidential election.

## KEY DATES

**1929** Presidency of Herbert Hoover.
Agricultural Marketing Act – set up Federal Farm Boards to encourage agricultural co-operatives.
Wall Street Crash – collapse of the Stock Market.
**1930** Hartley–Smoot tariff.
**1931** Repudiation of foreign debts.
National Credit Corporation set up – to lend funds to banks in distress.
**1932** Federal Home Loan Bank Act – to ease credit to save mortgages.
Reconstruction Finance Corporation set up – to lend funds to rescue companies in distress.

## 1 Introduction

> In Hoover we trusted
> And now we are busted

In the 1928 presidential election campaign, it is doubtful whether anyone could have beaten Herbert Hoover. In the 1932 campaign, he was generally vilified and had little chance of success. He was a tragic figure, prematurely aged and the butt throughout the country of cruel jokes such as the hitch-hikers' placards which read, 'If you don't give me a ride, I'll vote for Hoover'.

In the 1928 campaign the main issues were the support of prohibition, the urban values and the Catholicism of the Democratic candidate, Al Smith. The economy was hardly an issue and, in any event, there was little difference between the candidates' policies. By way of complete contrast, in 1932 the economy dominated. However, while in 1928 Hoover received 21,392,190 popular votes to Smith's 15,016,443, in 1932 Hoover's opponent, Franklin Delano Roosevelt, received 22,800,000 votes to 15,750,000. This was actually a fairly respectable result when one considers the attacks on Hoover, his lack-lustre campaign compared to Roosevelt's sparkle, and the fact that the election result seemed prejudged by most people; Hoover himself said, 'As we expected we were defeated in the election.'

Clearly the issue that destroyed President Hoover was the Depression and his inability to deal with it with any degree of success. In this chapter we will consider why he seemingly failed so completely. To aid our understanding it is important to consider Hoover's background and attitudes before going on to look at the depth of the problems which faced him and how he responded to them. We need also to examine the 1932 election campaign to see what, if anything, his opponent was offering the American people that Hoover had not. Finally, because Hoover has been called 'the last of the old Presidents and the first of the new', we need to investigate what is meant by this remark and consider how far it is justified by his response to the Depression.

## 2 Herbert Hoover, His Background and Beliefs

> **KEY ISSUE** What beliefs did Herbert Hoover bring with him to the presidency?

If any one deserved to be President then that person surely was Herbert Hoover. Rarely has anyone been so well qualified for the task or had so much confidence placed in his ability. Hoover encapsulated the American Dream. Born in 1874 and orphaned by the age of nine, he was raised by his uncle in a small rural settlement in Oregon. He learnt mining engineering at Stanford University and gained a reputation for excellence as an engineer. He became a millionaire before he was 35 years old. He believed passionately in the values of hard work and enterprise. He once said that 'if a man has not made a million by the time he's forty he is not worth much'. Yet he was humanitarian too. Based in London when war was declared in August 1914, he headed the American Citizens' Relief Committee, arranging for thousands of compatriots caught up in war zones to be repatriated. He later went on to head the Commission for Relief in Belgium where he made massive efforts to ensure victims of the conflict received necessary aid. When the USA entered the war in 1917, Hoover became Food Administrator and such was his success that American farmers produced surpluses with which it was possible to feed the hungry in war-torn Europe. His reputation was such that both major parties were considering him as a possible presidential candidate before, in 1920, he chose the Republicans. Defeated by Harding in the contest for candidate, he became Secretary for Commerce in his administration and quickly made his mark as a tireless worker. In fact, he became so influential that he was called 'Secretary of Commerce and undersecretary of everything else'. Coolidge kept him on but privately referred to him as 'the boy wonder' and later disparagingly said of him, 'That man has offered me unsolicited advice for six years and all of it bad'. This was simply not true. Among other things, Coolidge had accepted his advice on the use of farm co-operatives rather than direct federal aid, the development of electric power by private industry and the use of the Labor Department to broker an end to industrial disputes. Hoover was shy and taciturn, uncomfortable with strangers and often shunned publicity. He was an administrator more than a politician and eschewed political games and infighting. He was respected rather than regarded with affection, but generally Americans had high expectations of his administration. After all, it seemed the economy was booming and as Secretary of Commerce, he was widely believed to have been one of the architects of the prosperity.

However, we need to go deeper than this thumbnail sketch of Hoover's early career. He was in a sense an ideologue. It was his tragedy that he could not shift from his fundamental beliefs which he acquired at an early age and never altered.

## a) Quakerism

Hoover was descended on both sides from old established Quaker families. For most of his life he and his wife were devout and practising Quakers. This instilled in Hoover two fundamental ways of thinking that are relevant to his handling of the Depression:

    i) A strong sense of discipline and duty. He believed in 'ordered freedom' – freedom disciplined by a will to put others' welfare before one's own and a willingness to co-operate with others to solve problems.

    ii) While he could accept that other belief systems allowed flexibility in their solutions to problems, Hoover himself believed in an unvarying 'Inner Light' which would expand to cover every new problem that arose. The 'Inner Light' was itself immutable and meant in practical terms that Hoover would not – could not – change his views to meet changing circumstances.

## b) 'American Individualism'

Hoover's political philosophy was spelt out in a book, 'American Individualism' published in 1922,[1] and from its ideas he hardly wavered. He believed above all in equality of opportunity. He was a self-made man; he felt everyone else could be too. Having said this, he did not support strictly laissez-faire policies, believing the government should co-ordinate the activities of capital and labour and a balance should be struck between individualism and the needs of the community. The book went on to examine the influence of religion, economic and political phases, and the future, but the emphasis was always on the responsibility of the individual and the curbing of excesses and exploitation. Hoover's philosophy was an intensely moral one. He had a very high view of human nature – perhaps too high. That he regarded 'American individualism' as the best system in the world is self-evident. He saw the role of government as facilitating its development.

# 3 The USA During the Great Depression

> **KEY ISSUE**  What economic and social effects did the Great Depression have on American life?

Economic statistics of the Depression are plentiful and tell their own story of the dramatic contraction in economic activity. However, they do not always illustrate the human cost, as statistics tend to be abstractions. For this reason, the economic effects and the human dimension will be separated in the following account. It is also important to consider why this particular depression bit so deeply and lasted so long. The USA was, after all, quite used to depressions as part of the normal economic cycle – a cycle which Herbert Hoover ironically was trying to break up so that prosperity would become the norm. These then will be the three issues considered in this section: the economic effects, the human cost, and why this depression was different from others.

## a) Economic Effects of the Great Depression

There are no totally reliable unemployment figures for this period because the federal government did not keep centralised records until the mid-1930s. However, there is no doubt that unemployment soared. One historian wrote that they resembled the casualty figures in the battles of the First World War. An official government source suggests unemployment rose from 3.2 per cent of the labour force in 1929 to 25.2 per cent by 1933; this meant that 12,830,000 were out of work. The Labor Research Association complained that these figures were underestimates and claimed that the real figure was nearer 17 million. Another source suggests that by 1933, 33 per cent of the workforce was unemployed. It has been estimated that the national wage bill in 1932 was only 40 per cent of the 1929 figure. However, the figures do not show the numbers in part-time and unofficial working and, as we shall see, the latter at least was quite significant.

Unemployment and underemployment were not evenly spread throughout the country. New York State alone had one million unemployed. In Ohio, the city of Cleveland had 50 per cent of its workforce unemployed and that of Toledo, a staggering 80 per cent. Afrocaribbeans and women fared particularly badly.

## i) Afro-caribbeans

'The Nation' reported in April 1931 that the number of afro-caribbeans out of work was four to six times higher than whites, and that poorly paid jobs traditionally reserved for afro-caribbeans such as those of waiter and lift attendant were now increasingly being offered to whites. Afro-caribbean rural workers, of course, were used to depressed conditions, but the migratory path to employment in the northern cities, opened during the 1920s, was now generally closed to them. One commentator from Georgia said, 'Most blacks did not even know the Great Depression had come. They always had been poor and only thought the whites were catching up'.

## ii) Women

Women fared badly too, particularly those of the working classes. Women in menial jobs were likely to be laid off before men, and those in domestic service suffered because families increasingly could no longer afford to keep them on. Married women whose wages were often needed to keep the family solvent were even accused of being responsible for male unemployment and it was quite common for them to be dismissed. In 1930 over 75 per cent of American school systems refused to employ married women.

There were some pockets of resistance to the onset of Depression. A local military base, state university or seat of state government could delay it, as could localised circumstances such as the temporary oil boom in Kigmore, Texas – which ironically led to a glut of oil and a collapse of prices in that industry. There were also 'depression-proof' industries such as cigarette manufacture. This helped Louisville and Richmond from feeling the worst effects of the Depression until later. By 1933, however, nowhere in the USA could escape its effects.

With fewer in productive work, the growth rate went into decline – from 6.7 per cent in 1929 to minus 14.7 per cent in 1932, representing a fall in Gross National Product (GNP) from $203.6 billion in 1929 to $144.2 billion in 1932. General price levels fell by 25 per cent during the period; farm prices fell by a half. Individual industries each have their own statistics of decline. In the coal industry, production in 1932 was the lowest since 1904 and the workforce fell by 300,000; many of those in work were only part-time and wages could be as low as $2.50 per day. 75 per cent of textile firms were losing money, while iron and steel production fell by 59 per cent and US Steel Corporation's workforce was wholly part-time by the end of 1932. Car sales fell from 4,455,178 in 1929 to 1,103,557 four years later. The average number of people employed in the 'motor city' of Detroit fell by 21.5 per cent between the last four months of 1928 and the last four months of 1929. In Toledo, Willis-Overland laid off 25,000 of their workforce between May 1929 and spring 1932, leaving a staff of only 3,000. In the meantime, the number employed by both

General Electric and Westerhouse making electrical appliances was more than halved; the only electric goods not to suffer a significant decline in demand were lightbulbs. The construction industry, already in decline before 1929, saw the number of residential units built fall 82 per cent between 1929 and 1932. Construction contracts were valued at $6.6 billion in 1929 and $1.3 billion three years later.

Credit had all but vanished. The Stock Market went into serious decline despite occasional rallies as in December 1929 and in April 1930. The index of industrial stocks fell from 220.1 in November 1929 to 196.1 by December 1930, 116.6 by December 1931 and 84.81 by December 1932. Bank failures proliferated. There had been 5,000 in the entire period 1921 to 1929, but there were over 10,000 between 1929 and 1933. Most of these were small banks that had overextended their lending in the times of prosperity and now could not meet their depositors' demands for their money. When farmers, for example, could not meet their mortgage repayments, the banks had to foreclose; in doing so, they lost liquid assets in the form of mortgage repayments and gained bankrupt, often unsaleable, farms in exchange. Under these circumstances, depositors often lost confidence in their bank and the resultant 'run' to withdraw their money would finish it off. Alternatively, many people simply needed the money they had in their accounts; they may have lost their job, have been on short-time working or have needed to meet a debt. If enough of them wanted their money at the same time, the result was the same; the collapse of the bank with the loss of their savings for all those depositors who did not withdraw them quickly enough.

By 1933 the USA was a land of hard cash, where those still in work fiercely protected their jobs, where credit was tight and no one was prepared to take a risk. It was also a land singularly unable to handle a major depression.

## b) Life in the Great Depression

### i) Unemployment

The USA was ill-equipped to handle unemployment. Very little provision was made. There was, for example, no federal unemployment benefit. The 'work ethic' was very prevalent in America and unemployment among the able bodied was generally held to be their own fault. For this reason alone, the psychological effects of mass unemployment were devastating. There are many cases of people pretending still to be in work, to go out early each morning with a briefcase or toolbag, packed lunch and the like – to keep up appearances. Dr Martin Bickham advocated work schemes instead of just relief in Chicago:

> It was simple. The man was not to earn more than would be required for his family to live. No more than he would be getting on relief,

though the pay was union scale. He'd work so many days until the equivalent sum was reached. The men wanted to work. This was the
5 dominant theme throughout all the years of the Depression. I seldom found a man who was willing to accept relief as a process of life. He knew it was debilitating. I'll never forget the morning we opened the office. It was a cold November day, 1930. Thousands of men were lined up for blocks. Many were skilled men and carried their tools with them.
10 In the course of that winter, we put ten thousand to work.

The strain on family life was intense. The number of marriages fell from 1.23 million in 1929 to 982,00 in 1932, with a concomitant fall in the birth rate from 21.2 per thousand in 1929 to 19.5 in 1932. Suicide rates increased greatly from 14 per 10,000 in 1929 to 17.4 in 1932.

## ii) Relief

The nature of relief varied greatly because it was provided variously by states, local authorities or charities, with the latter providing the largest percentage. In fact, before 1932 no state had any system of recognised unemployment insurance and only 11 operated any kind of pension scheme – with a total outlay of only $220,000, aiding a mere 1,000 people. At a time when the population was ageing, the majority of elderly people lived below the poverty line. With very few private pension schemes – in 1925 only 36,000 pensioners were in receipt of benefits from 500 pension plans – old people traditionally either had to keep working, live on their savings, or rely on their children for support. The Depression meant that in the main, these options were no longer viable. Often to obtain any measure of relief, one had to sell all one's possessions, use up all one's savings, and become literally destitute. The stigma of doing so was deliberately intended to dissuade people from applying; ten states disenfranchised applicants and some churches even banned recipients of relief from attending their services. 'Fortune' magazine showed that only 25 per cent of those entitled to relief actually received any. Single people and childless couples were very unlikely to receive anything.

## iii) Hoboes

Many of the unemployed became 'hoboes' – homeless wanderers seeking any kind of work. By 1932, it was estimated that there were between one and two million of them, many of whom lived in shanty towns on the outskirts of settlements. Hoboes were usually given a hard time. The Southern Pacific Railroad claimed to have thrown 68,300 of them from its trains. The state of California posted guards to turn them away at its borders and in Atlanta, Georgia, they were put into chain gangs (groups of prisoners chained together while working outside the prison, for example in digging roadside drainage ditches). However, with the passage of time hoboes did become a new

Unemployed waiting for admission to the New York Municipal
Lodging House, 1930

type of hero in American mythology. The following account of life as a hobo was given by Louis Banks:

1  Black and white, it didn't make any difference who you were 'cause everybody was poor. All friendly, sleep in a jungle. We used to take a big pot and cook food, meat and beans all together. We all set together, we made a tent. Twenty five or thirty would be out on the side of the

5  rail, white and colored. They didn't have no mothers and sisters, they didn't have no home, they were dirty, they had overalls on, they didn't have no food, they didn't have anything.

    Sometimes we sent one hobo to walk, to see if there were any jobs open. He'd come back and say: Detroit, no jobs. He'd say: they're hirin'

10  in New York City. Sometimes ten or fifteen of us would be on the train. And I'd hear one of 'em holler. He'd fall off, he'd get killed. . . .

    And then I saw a railroad police, a white police. They call him Texas Slim. He shoots you off all trains. We come out of Lima, Ohio. Lima Slim, he would kill you if he catch you on any train. Sheep train or any

15  kind of merchandise train. He would shoot you off, he wouldn't ask you to get off.

    I was in chain gangs and been in jail all over the country. I was in a chain gang in Georgia. I had to pick cotton for four months, for just hoboin' on a train. . . .

20  A man had to be on the road. Had to leave his wife, had to leave his mother, leave his family just to try to get money to live on. But he think: my dear mother, tryin' to send her money, worryin' how she's starvin'.

## iv) The Strain on Resources

For those who should have received relief, there was the added problem that the sources were running out of funds. Charities naturally suffer a decline in revenue during a depression, at the very time there is most pressure on their funds. States too received less in taxes as unemployment rose. As a result, many had to cut rather than expand their services. In Arkansas, for example, schools were closed for ten months in the year, while teachers in Chicago went unpaid during the winter of 1932–3. The simple truth was that charities could supply only 6 per cent of necessary funds in 1932, and states and local government agencies could not even begin to provide the shortfall of 94 per cent. In fact, in the years 1931 and 1932 when demand was greatest, most cut their relief appropriations. Michigan, for example, reduced funds from $2 million in 1931 to $832,000 in 1932. The inevitable result was that many people were hungry and starving. Fortune magazine again estimated in September 1932 that as much as 28 per cent of the total population was receiving no income – and this estimate did not include the 11 million farm workers, many of whom were in acute difficulties.

## v) In the Countryside

According to US Department of Agriculture statistics, 58 farms in every thousand changed hands in 1929, of which 19.5 were forced sales. By 1936 this figure had risen to 76.6, of which 41.7 were forced. Often the auction of foreclosed farm property attracted violence. But there were other ways in which those repossessing property could be thwarted. Local farmers would agree only to bid a few cents and then return the farm to its former owner. Sometimes there was intimidation. Two state governors said that payments on farm mortgages could be postponed until circumstances improved.

## vi) Poverty in the Midst of Plenty

The tragedy was that people went hungry in one of the richest food producing countries in the world. Farm prices were so low that food could not be profitably harvested. In Montana, for example, wheat was rotting in the fields. Nor were meat prices sufficient to warrant transporting animals to market. In Oregon, sheep were slaughtered and left to the buzzards. In Chicago meanwhile, women scoured rubbish tips for anything edible. Total relief funds in that city amounted to only $100,000 per day, which worked out at payments of only $2.40 per adult and $1.50 per child recipient per week. In 1931 there were 3.8 million one-parent families headed by a woman, with only 19,280 receiving any aid.

# 4 Why the Depression Lasted So Long

> **KEY ISSUE** Why couldn't the Great Depression be brought to an end?

Various explanations have been given for the duration of the Depression, although they are usually closely interconnected:

## a) Foreign Economic Crises

Herbert Hoover always blamed foreign economies for the Depression. It was their weakness, he felt, that stifled trade and as we shall see, many of his measures to combat the Depression were intended to strengthen foreign economies. While many historians would go along with his analysis up to a point, there is criticism that the USA, as the richest country in the world, had not, in the 1920s, assumed a dominant role as world economic leader. American tariffs, one should remember, restricted international trade, and were to do so even more ferociously after the Hawley–Smoot tariff in 1930. In particular, the USA is criticised for not devaluing its currency when others were losing value, thus making American goods even more expensive for foreigners.

## b) The Nature of American Business

The vast growth of the American economy came during the years following the Civil War when the country underwent a major process of industrialisation and rapidly settled the continent. However, government non-intervention meant that industries often came under the control of individuals or small groups who could control wages, prices and output to maximise their profits. While, on the surface, the system was highly competitive and dominated by market forces, in reality it was controlled by trusts and cartels. Inevitably these two forces – of free and controlled markets – would one day collide. The tension between them had, in the past, been masked by the growing population and territorial expansion that created enormous demand. However, when these ended the country was left with a problem of overproduction and excess capacity. Relatively low wages and the unequal spread of prosperity, for example, meant that the population was consuming less than it should and that, unless new forms of demand could be found, the economy would continue to stagnate.

## c) The Totality of the Depression

Economic depressions are often unevenly distributed throughout a country. Some industries remain unscathed; others may even benefit. Some areas of the country escape. However, the totality of the Great Depression meant that no sector remained immune. This was to have two major effects that led to the Depression being prolonged. Firstly, there was the absence of alternative employment opportunities. Every country which has gone through an Industrial Revolution finds its old industries – coal, iron and steel, and textiles – lose their competitive edge in the face of competition from rivals whose more recent industrialisation means that their methods of production are more modern and efficient. However, as the old industries contract accordingly, the workforce can normally expect to find employment in the newer industries such as car manufacturing and the manufacture of electrical appliances. But, as we have seen, because of overproduction and underconsumption, these industries were hit particularly badly during the Depression in the USA. As a result, employment opportunities were no longer available in them either. Clearly, this prolonged the Depression. The allied point is the geographical totality of the Depression. Farmers, for example, had largely been depressed throughout the 1920s and so their purchasing power was poor. Because both rural and urban areas suffered neither could help the other.

## d) Lack of Government Expansion

A group of radical economists including Rexford Tugwell and Adolph

Berle (later to be important supporters of Franklin D. Roosevelt) argued that the Depression was caused by the unequal distribution of production and spending under unregulated capitalism. Put simply, too many goods were being produced and too few consumers could afford to buy them. A Brookings Institute Report of 1934, for example, showed that 8 per cent of families had earned 42 per cent of the national wealth, while 60 per cent earned only 23 per cent. If the capitalist economy could not maintain a balance between the power of consumption and earnings, then, it was argued, the government should intervene to do so. This clearly would involve a far greater role to be played by government – by increasing taxation of the rich, for example, to help equalise income, and with the increased revenue to undertake public works to increase employment and 'kick start' the economy. In the USA, of course, the prevailing government policies had been the opposite of this, with retrenchment and balancing the budget being seen as priorities.

## e) Monetarist Theories

Associated in particular with the work of Milton Friedman in the 1970s, monetarist theories hold that a decline in the stock of money often foreshadows a depression. Failure to increase the stock of money will prolong the depression as people have less money to spend. Altogether, the amount of money in circulation fell by about 33 per cent during the years 1929–33. Monetarists, meanwhile, have argued that a 3 per cent to 5 per cent annual increase is necessary to achieve a comparable rate of economic growth. Friedman argued, for example, that in October 1931 the rise in the discount rate from 1.5 to 3.5 per cent caused a 25 per cent fall in industrial production over the next year. According to monetarists, in other words, the tight monetary policy pursued by the Federal Reserve Board stifled recovery.

There is undoubtedly a large measure of truth in each of these explanations. Which do you find the most persuasive? Together they show that the Depression was a highly complex phenomenon with no easy solutions. However, increasingly, the federal government was expected to find the answers.

## 5 Federal Government Policies

> **KEY ISSUE**  How did President Hoover's administration try to tackle the Great Depression?

President Hoover worked tirelessly to combat the Depression. As he left office in 1933 his face was lined and drawn. He worried constantly, had a humanitarian concern for suffering and misery and gave generously to charity. He cut his own and state officials' salaries by 20 per cent to help provide revenues for his recovery measures. His working hours were long; after rising before 6 am and exercising with trusted advisers with a medicine ball, no doubt discussing important issues as the ball was thrown to and fro, he worked all day and long into the night with scarcely a break for meals. He well understood the seriousness of the Depression which overshadowed all but the first seven months of his presidency. In public, however, he had to be optimistic in the face of such adversity; this has led many to argue that he quite lost touch with reality. When, for example, he told the press that unemployment was falling, this created considerable resentment among many of the jobless who could thereby have been regarded by others as too lazy to get a job. As a result of his constant public hopefulness, Hoover gradually lost all credibility. 'Hoovervilles' – the shanties were hoboes lived – were named after him as were 'hoover blankets' – the newspapers in which they wrapped themselves to keep warm. The anger and sense of betrayal that was directed against him personally is well exemplified in this parody of Psalm 23:

1 Hoover is my shepherd, I am in want. He maketh me to lie down in park benches. He restoreth my doubt in the Republican Party. He leadeth me in the path of destruction for his party's sake.
  Yea, though I walk through the valley of destruction, I fear evil: For thou
5 art with me: the politicians and professors, they frighten me.
  Thou preparest a reduction in my salary before me in the presence of my Creditors; Thou anointest my income with taxes; my expenses runneth over.
  Surely unemployment and poverty will follow me all the days of the
10 Republican administration:
  And I shall dwell in a mortgaged house forever.

Hoover's problem was that he could not abandon his two central tenets of self-help and voluntary co-operation. Having said this, he did more and involved the government more in the economy than any other President in history had. However, he could not countenance what many increasingly argued was necessary – direct government relief. He continued to believe that the economy had to right itself. 'Economic depression,' he said, 'cannot be cured by legislative action or executive pronouncement. Economic wounds must be healed by the action of the cells of the economic body – the producers and consumers themselves.'

Hoover certainly understood the need for the government to take action to facilitate this. He gave short shrift, for example, to the advice of his Treasury Secretary, Andrew Mellon, who was advising businessmen still solvent to fire their workers and sell everything until the crisis was over. Hoover called these ideas 'childlike' and was eventually to remove Mellon from his post by sending him to London as ambassador. However, as we shall see, Hoover's policies were simply not far reaching enough to address anywhere near adequately the depth of the Depression. He was prepared to do something, but nowhere near enough.

## a) Agriculture

Hoover called a special session of Congress in April 1929, before the Wall Street Crash, to deal with the pressing problems of agriculture. He would no more accept the McNary-Haugen proposals than his predecessors, but he was prepared to help farmers to help themselves. The Agricultural Marketing Act, 1929, established a nine-person Federal Farm Board with funds of $500 million to create farmers' marketing co-operatives called 'stabilisation corps'. These were to be given the task of storing and eventually disposing of farm surpluses in an orderly way. However, they had no power to order restrictions in production and huge surpluses in 1931 and 1932 both at home and abroad saw prices plummet. The Grain Stabilisation Corporation, for example, bought wheat in Chicago at 80c a bushel while the world price had fallen to 60c. By the time it ceased its purchases in summer, 1931, it had paid an average of 82c per bushel for 300 million bushels while the world price had fallen to 40c a bushel. The Corporation might have been helping farmers but it was also accused of throwing taxpayers' money away. It was purchasing farm produce at well over the market price and therefore was seen to encourage farmers to keep producing more, when, in fact, they should have been encouraged to produce less. By 1932 the world price of wheat was between 30c and 39c a bushel, less than harvesting costs in the USA. When Congress did propose a bill to subsidise farmers to reduce production, Hoover threatened to veto it because it undermined the principle of voluntary action. In the event, the bill failed without any need for a veto. It was too radical a measure for the time.

The agricultural policy failed mainly, then, for two reasons:

i) Because it was paying American farmers artificially high prices and this could not continue in the long term;

ii) Because it treated agriculture as a domestic issue and, therefore, failed to take account of foreign considerations. Without high tariffs, there was little point in trying to keep the American price artificially high. The answer to the problem of cheap foreign imports, then, seemed to be even higher tariffs.

## b) Tariffs

The Hawley–Smoot tariff, which came into force in June 1930, was the highest in American history with average duties of 40 per cent on both agricultural and industrial items. It led to most European nations abandoning free trade and to even fewer American goods being exported. This, of course, was of no advantage to farmers with their huge surpluses. Knowing this, farming interests in Congress fought hard against the measure, and it passed the Senate by only two votes. Hoover could have vetoed the bill but chose not to.

## c) Repudiation of War Debts

Hoover blamed the Depression on Europe but he was probably wrong to do so. It was the American Depression that spread to Europe and not vice versa. Certainly after the Wall Street Crash, American credit dried up. The Hawley-Smoot tariff made things worse. In the years 1929 and 1930 the value of international trade fell in total by $500 million and in the following year it fell by $1.2 billion.

Germany was particularly affected by the demise of American credit. When the German government became virtually bankrupt it announced the suspension of reparations payments and said that it might also have to default on loans. Hoover feared a war over this. He knew that the French, in particular, might resort to military action to get their reparations. Moreover, defaulting on debts would adversely affect American banks which were already struggling to keep solvent. On 21 June 1931 Hoover announced the USA would defer the collection of its debts for 18 months if other countries would do the same. This, he hoped, would release monies for investment. In the event, it was too little too late to arrest the collapse of European economies. Interestingly, however, when the 'moratorium' came up for renewal in December 1932, it was during the period of Hoover's 'lame duck' presidency, before the new incumbent, Roosevelt took over. He advised the latter to continue the moratorium. However, Roosevelt, sensing hostility in Congress, agreed to the passage of the Johnson Act that made it illegal to sell in the USA the securities of any country which had reneged on its debts. As the Stock Market was still moribund, this had little effect except to make European countries even more resentful of the USA. Finland was the only country that continued to pay its debts. Hoover also had great hopes of a projected London Economic Conference but, again, by the time it took place in 1933 he was no longer President.

## d) Voluntarism

At first, Hoover hoped to persuade businessmen and state governments to continue as if there was no Depression – to solve it through their own voluntary efforts. He called meetings of businessmen in which he implored them not to reduce their workforce or cut wages, but rather to maintain their output and urge people to buy. He encouraged state leaders to begin new programmes of public works as well as continuing with the old. However, as the Depression worsened, business had little choice but to retrench. Workers were laid off, most investment was postponed, and wages were reduced. As we have seen, states also had to cut back. The problems were simply too great for voluntarism to work, particularly when it went against customary business practice. Bankers, for example, set up the National Credit Corporation in October 1931 with the task of helping failing banks survive. It began with a capital fund of $500 million donated by the major financial institutions. However, at a time when banks continued to fail at unprecedented rates, by the end of 1931, the Corporation had spent only $10 million. Bankers were simply too ingrained in their ways to begin investing in failing concerns. The Corporation died a death, showing again that individual financial concerns would almost always put their own interests before those of their country.

## e) Unemployment Relief

Hoover secured additional appropriations from Congress to the tune of $500 million in 1932 to help the various agencies give relief. However, this was wholly inadequate to meet the scale of the problem. He set up the President's Emergency Committee for Employment to help the agencies to organise their efforts. But, again, he would not countenance direct federal relief, arguing this destroyed self-help and created a class of people dependent on the government for handouts. Even during the severe drought of 1930–31, which saw near starvation conditions in much of the South, he balked at direct relief. In the end, Congress allocated a pitifully small sum, $47 million, and even that was to be offered as loans that must be later repaid.

## f) Federal Home Loan Bank Act

This measure, passed in July 1932, was intended to save mortgages by making credit easier. A series of Federal Home Loan banks was set up to help loan associations providing mortgages. However, as the maximum loan was only 50 per cent of the value of the property it was largely ineffective. It was simply another example of help that failed because it was inadequate to deal with the seriousness of the situation – in this case homes being repossessed.

## g) Reconstruction Finance Corporation (RFC)

This was undoubtedly Hoover's most radical measure to combat the Depression and was a forerunner of the New Deal initiatives of Franklin D. Roosevelt. The Reconstruction Finance Corporation was established in January 1932 with authority to lend up to $2 billion to rescue banks, insurance companies, railroads and construction companies in distress. The new Treasury Secretary, Ogden Mills said the RFC was 'an insurance measure more than anything else'. It was designed to restore confidence particularly in financial institutions.

Of its loans, 90 per cent went to small and medium banks, and 70 per cent to banks in towns of less than 5,000 population. However, critics of the RFC pointed to the size of individual loans not the actual number. They argued that 50 per cent of loans went to the 7 per cent of borrowers who happened to be the biggest banks and, of the first $61 million committed by the RFC, $41 million was loaned to no more than three institutions. One alone, the Central Republican National Bank and Trust Company, received $90 million. This came soon after the return to the bank of its President – who had been seconded to run the RFC. The $90 million, incidentally, was almost as much as the bank held in total deposits at the time. Similarly, the biggest loans also went to the biggest railroads and public utilities. The government argued its case by saying that the largest firms were the biggest employers so it made sense to help them in the war against unemployment. However, many critics saw the RFC as giving direct relief to large concerns while none was offered to individuals in distress. In fact, the clamour for direct relief became so great that in summer 1932 Hoover finally agreed in some measure. He gave his support to the Emergency Relief and Construction Act which authorised the RFC to lend up to $1.5 billion to states to finance public works. However, to be eligible the states had to declare virtual bankruptcy and the works undertaken had to produce revenues which would eventually pay off the loans. When Hoover agreed to this, many of his erstwhile supporters felt he had gone too far. In 1932 James M. Beck, a former Solicitor General, compared Hoover's government to that of Soviet Russia! Many members of the Republican Party believed strongly in policies of non-intervention.

However, in the end, the RFC offered far too little far too late. By this time, in the words of Calvin Coolidge's former secretary, Edward Clark, 'Today, there seems to be no class nor section where Hoover is strong or where a decision is respected because [he] made it'. Why do you think this was? Why did the policies outlined above not work? Hoover's credibility which was already severely damaged was finally destroyed by his role in an event that made him seem cruel as well as unfeeling. This was the treatment of the 'Bonus Army'.

## h) War Veterans and the Bonus Army

Ironically, it was Hoover who had set up the Veterans' Administration for those who had seen military service. Annual federal expenditure on veteran's disabilities was $675.8 million. However, Hoover will always be remembered for what happened to the 'Bonus Army'. Congress had agreed a veteran's 'bonus' in 1925. Based on the number of years of service, it was to be paid in full to each veteran in 1945. But, quite understandably, as the Depression hit many veterans said they needed it now. A march to Washington was organised to publicise their cause. By 15 June 1932, 20,000 people were camped in the capital, mainly around the

Anacostia Flats region. On that day the House of Representatives voted by 226 votes to 175 to allow immediate payment of the bonus. Largely because of the cost, two days later the Senate vetoed this. Feeling for their plight, but sure that nothing could be done for them, Hoover offered $100,000 to pay for their transportation home. However, many refused to budge. Some were squatting in derelict buildings in Pennsylvania Avenue with the tacit support of the district Police Superintendent who was sympathetic to their cause. Hoover increasingly feared violence and even revolution. The White House was protected with barricades and its gates were chained. The Secretary of War, determined to move the squatters, called in troops under General Douglas MacArthur. Tanks and infantry not only shifted the squatters but chased them back to the main camp on Anacostia Flats where tear gas was used to disperse them. The camp was destroyed, many marchers were injured, and two babies died from the effects of the gas. A War Department official publicly called these men who had served their country, 'Tramps and hoodlums with a generous sprinkling of Communist agitators'. Although MacArthur had gone beyond his authority in attacking the camp on Anacostia Flats, the deed was done and Hoover came out in his support. Later, in the election campaign he even blurted out, 'Thank God you have a government that knows how to deal with a mob'. However, Americans had been horrified at the scenes and whether they were his fault or not, Hoover was blamed. The violent dispersal of the Bonus Army by the military was a major political blunder.

# 6 The 1932 Presidential Election

> **KEY ISSUES** What were the alternatives to Republican policies in 1932, and why did Franklin D. Roosevelt win the presidential election of that year?

## a) Radical Alternatives

The depths of the Depression undoubtedly led some to wonder whether the American system could survive. Extremism usually thrives on hopelessness and despair, and there was certainly enough of both during the Depression. However, there is very little evidence that the USA was anywhere near revolution and, unlike in European countries, extremist parties never received more than a small amount of support.

### i) The Extreme Right

There were the beginnings of an American Fascist movement, called the Silver Shirts. Despite the increasing interest shown in it by disaffected members of the Ku Klux Klan, its membership was estimated to be less than 700. Certainly its effects at this time were insignificant.

## ii) The Extreme Left

American Communists expected the Depression to lead to revolution. They set up Unemployment Councils with the slogan, 'Fight – Don't Starve' and organised marches against unemployment. They were a small, highly disciplined party in the revolutionary tradition of underground activity. They took their orders from Moscow which had insisted they refuse to work with Socialists or any non-communist organisation. Moscow also had little understanding of the USA and some of the orders it gave demonstrated this. Afro-caribbeans, for example, were viewed as a suppressed nationality and the Party was persuaded to campaign for the creation of a separate afro-caribbean state in those parts of the south-east where they were in the majority. Even when they did work with afro-caribbeans to improve their living standards as in the Sharecroppers' Union, set up in 1931, their efforts were defeated by the officially condoned violence and intimidation that destroyed the members' will to fight. During the 1932 presidential election the Communists spent much of their time sniping at the Socialists. This helped to account for their poor showing in the election.

The decade of the 1920s was a difficult one for the Socialists. They had lost the support of many intellectuals over their opposition to American entry into the First World War and had split with the Communists in 1919. They had been weakened by the 'Red Scare' of that year, and they were committed to working with the American Federation of Labour (AFL) which was conservative and often racist in nature. In the 1932 election the Socialist candidate, Norman Thomas, polled fewer than one million votes. Many of his own supporters felt it was more important to defeat Hoover than to vote for Socialism. Many gave their support to Franklin D. Roosevelt simply for that reason. To others Roosevelt really did symbolise new hope, offering the real change they were clamouring for.

## b) Franklin Delano Roosevelt

Roosevelt was born into one of the most prestigious families in the USA, tracing his roots back to the first Dutch settlers in the area of modern-day New York. He had a fairly idyllic upbringing on the family estate at Hyde Park in New York State. He was educated at the prestigious school of Groton, going on to Harvard University where he was popular without excelling himself academically. He trained to be a lawyer, but was to invest far more energy in the social whirl. His passion was sailing. In 1905 he married his distant cousin, Eleanor, a niece of President Theodore Roosevelt. He entered politics as a Democrat in 1910 when he fought for a seat in the New York Senate mainly because his promoters had been looking for someone who could finance himself. Benefiting from infighting among his New York colleagues, he climbed the slippery pole of state politics with relative ease. In 1913 he was offered the post of Assistant Secretary of the Navy where he gained a reputation for enthusiasm and competence. In the 1920 presidential election he was nominated as Democratic candidate for the vice-presidency. That battle lost, he was struck down one year later by the disease which paradoxically may have been responsible for all his later energy, optimism and dynamism. He caught polio, then a killer disease. However, with the unfailing support of his wife, Roosevelt survived, although he was never to walk again except with the aid of painful braces. Through most of the 1920s he recuperated, grounded himself thoroughly in politics, and evinced a new determination to make something of himself.

In 1928 Roosevelt became Governor of New York State. He was noted as a reformer – he modernised the state's penal system, for example, building new prisons and revising harsh penalties – and for appointing able people to office rather than political cronies. However, it was with the onset of the Depression that he really came into his own. No intellectual himself, he was always ready to listen to those who were, and during his second term of office as governor he set up the 'Brains' Trust'. This was headed by academics, notable among whom were Raymond Moley, Rexford Tugwell, Adolph Berle and Felix Frankfurter. Many of them would remain with Roosevelt throughout the rest of his career. If it was they who convinced him that the government should intervene directly to combat the Depression, Roosevelt already had a proactive reputation of intervention in New York. In particular, he had broken with tradition by setting up the Temporary Emergency Relief Administration in 1932. This was given $20 million, financed from an increase in income tax, for work relief during winter 1931. The name of the organisation is significant. Roosevelt saw these kinds of agency very much as temporary expedients to meet a crisis. It was nevertheless the first state-run relief effort in the nation. In what ways do you think Roosevelt's policies, as a presidential candidate, would be different from Hoover's? Why do you think this would be?

## c) The Election Campaigns

Roosevelt was by far the strongest Democratic nominee for candidate. Hoover was the only possible Republican nominee unless the Party changed its policies. However, Hoover was too wrapped up in fighting the Depression to campaign effectively. The members of his re-election team were themselves short on ideas. One slogan they thought up but dared not suggest to the candidate was 'Boy! wasn't that some Depression'. Hoover generally had poor relations with the press: Roosevelt courted them. Hoover had never had much charisma: Roosevelt exuded it. However, many historians have argued that there was little to choose between the candidates in terms of economic policies. Certainly, Roosevelt did not promise government action to solve economic problems. In fact, he even made a speech on 19 October attacking Hoover's 'extravagant government spending' and pledging a 25 per cent cut in the federal budget.

The most important factor seems to have been that Hoover expected to lose, while his opponent was determined to win. Many of Roosevelt's promises were vague and even contradictory. In San Francisco he made a speech advocating economic regulation only as a last resort, while, at Oglethorpe University, Georgia, he spoke of bold experimentation to beat the Depression and of a redistribution of national income. However, Roosevelt did say things which captured the public imagination. In April 1932, before his nomination, he called, in a national radio address, for government to help 'the forgotten man'. In his acceptance speech, having received the nomination he repeated this idea:

1   On the farms, in the large, metropolitan areas, in the smaller cities and in the villages, millions of our citizens cherish the hope that their old standards of living and of thought have not gone forever. These millions cannot and shall not hope in vain.
5      I pledge you, I pledge myself, to a new deal for the American people. Let us all here assembled constitute ourselves prophets of a new order of competence and of courage. This is more than a political campaign; it is a call to arms. Give me your help, not to win votes alone but to aim in this crusade to restore America to its own people.

In this speech Roosevelt gave a name to his programme – 'The New Deal'. Traditionally the victorious nominee waited at home for the Party elders to visit him to offer him the nomination. However, Roosevelt took the unprecedented step of flying to Chicago, where the convention was being held, to accept it. This had the effect of showing to the rest of the USA that here was a man who meant business, who recognised there was a grave crisis and could not wait to get on with the job of solving it. Roosevelt used the radio to great effect. It was as though he was speaking directly to individuals. Hoover was by comparison merely boring. One might say there was no contest. Roosevelt won by the biggest majority since Abraham Lincoln in 1864. However, it was not a rout – 57 per cent of the popular vote is little more than half. Moreover, few really knew what Roosevelt stood for. Political columnist Walter Lippmann was possibly close to the truth when he wrote that Roosevelt was 'a pleasant man who, without any important qualifications for the office, would very much like to be President'.[2] However, Americans were voting above all for change. Whatever Roosevelt did stand for, this, above all, is what he seemed to offer.

# 7 President Hoover – an Epitaph

> **KEY ISSUE** An evaluation of Hoover's presidency.

Historians have recently been more sympathetic to Hoover. He has been viewed in particular as a victim both of his own mindset and of one of the most difficult to solve crises in American history. But, whereas Roosevelt was prepared to listen to ideas and to show flexibility, Hoover never altered. This was his biggest failing. He would consider many remedies, but he would not countenance direct federal intervention. He saw the government as a facilitator not as a creator. He believed it was the job of the government to provide the circumstances within which self-help and community responsibility could thrive. In doing this much, particularly during the Depression, Hoover did involve the government in more areas of life than ever before. Examples of this can be seen in the expansion of federal lending and encouragement of public works' schemes. However, Hoover's legislation was limited because he would not countenance direct government action at a time when it was desperately needed. As a result, what he offered fell far short of what was necessary. However, it must be remembered that neither Congress nor the business community were advocating wholesale federal government involvement either. Indeed, as government spending went into deficit partly as a result of measures he had taken, there was a widespread belief among both that Hoover should concentrate on balancing the budget.

Hoover was no exponent of laissez-faire. He believed that the government should be a positive force for good in society. It should facilitate, for example, equality of opportunity and moral rectitude in its citizens. Unfortunately, Hoover's principal philosophies of voluntarism and self-help were wholly inadequate to meet the magnitude of the crisis facing the USA when he was President. Nevertheless, as we have seen, his vision of the role of government was far in excess of that of his immediate predecessors. In this respect, Hoover may well be described as the 'first of the new Presidents' and 'the last of the old'. How would you evaluate him as President?

## References

1   H. Hoover, *American Individualism* (Doubleday, Page and Co, 1922).
2   Quoted in M. Parrish, *Anxious Decades* (W W Norton and Co, 1992), p. 285.

## Summary diagram
President Hoover and the Great Depression

| Year | Economic factors and statistics | Government action |
|------|--------------------------------|-------------------|
| 1929 | Unemployment 3.2%<br>GNP $203.6 billion<br>Growth rate 6.7%<br>October 1929, price of shares<br>fell by $14 billion | Agricultural Marketing Act |
| 1930 | Unemployment 8.9%<br>GNP $183.5 billion<br>Growth rate −9.6%<br>Serious drought SE of Rockies | Voluntarism, e.g. conferences<br>to try to dissuade business<br>from laying off workers.<br>Hawley–Smoot Tariff.<br>$49 million given in loans<br>to victims of the drought. |
| 1931 | Unemployment 16.3%<br>GNP $169.5 million<br>Growth rate −7.6% | Moratorium on collection of<br>war debts for 18 months.<br>National Credit Corporation.<br>set up with capital fund of<br>$500 million. |
| 1932 | Unemployment 24.1%<br>GNP $144.2 billion<br>Growth rate −14.7% | Federal Home Loan Bank Act.<br>Reconstruction Finance<br>Corporation set up with funds<br>of $2 billion.<br>Emergency Relief and<br>Construction Act.<br>Dispersal by force of 'Bonus<br>Army'. |

1932 Presidential Election

| Herbert Hoover | Franklin Delano Roosevelt |
|----------------|---------------------------|
| Self-help<br>Voluntarism<br>Community responsibility | 'New Deal for the<br>American People'<br>Restoration of confidence<br>in the USA |
| 15.7 million votes | 22.8 million votes |

## Working on Chapter 5

This chapter has attempted to do four things:

**i)** To consider the background and beliefs of President Hoover (section 2).
**ii)** To consider the nature and severity of the problems which he faced (sections 3 and 4).
**iii)** To consider how he responded to these problems (section 5).
**iv)** To consider why he was defeated by Franklin D. Roosevelt in the 1932 presidential election (sections 6 and 7).

In your note-making, you should think in particular about i) the values and beliefs Hoover brought to the presidency, ii) the extent of the problems caused by the Depression, and iii) how adequate his policies were to address them. In evaluating Hoover's presidency, you could consider how far Hoover's beliefs were reflected in his practice as President and why his efforts to combat the Depression were doomed to failure. This should lead you into an assessment of why Roosevelt was such an attractive alternative. You could also compile two charts:

a) Comparing the strong points of Roosevelt with those of Hoover.
b) Comparing the weak points of Roosevelt with those of Hoover.

The overall purpose of your notes in this chapter should be to show why Hoover's policies were insufficient to meet the Depression and why Roosevelt defeated him in the 1932 election.

## Answering essay questions on Chapter 5

Specific questions on Hoover usually concentrate on his handling of the Depression:

**1.** Why did Herbert Hoover easily win the 1928 presidential election but lose the 1932 one?

This question requires you to contrast the USA of 1932 with that of 1928. Many Americans had come to expect prosperity to be the norm in 1928 and they associated this prosperity with Republican government. By 1932, however, with the USA still deep in the grip of the Depression, the Republican policies seemed spent and useless. Most of the essay needs to deal with the failure of Hoover to combat the Depression effectively. You could also include something about the two elections. In 1928 the Democratic vote was hampered by public distrust of Al Smith because he was a Catholic and represented, it was felt, big city interests. In 1932 Roosevelt's charisma and energy contrasted sharply with Hoover's fatigue and lacklustre campaign.

**2.** Why did the policies of President Hoover fail to fight the Great Depression effectively?

This question requires knowledge of Hoover's policies but you also need to focus on their limitations, particularly in the light of the extent of the Depression. In particular, you will need to consider the issue of direct government intervention that Hoover was not prepared to adopt.

There are questions on the whole period of Republican government:

**3.** Account for the Republican dominance of government in the period 1921 to 1932.

This question requires you to consider the apparent prosperity of the years up to 1929, highlighting the general optimism and belief that it was due to Republican policies which helped business expansion. Hoover, it should be remembered, was elected in 1928, at the height, it seemed, of prosperity.

We have already considered some questions on the causes of the Great Depression but some ask you about its longevity:

**4.** Why did the Great Depression which followed the Wall Street Crash of 1929 last so long?

This is primarily an economic history question which requires knowledge of the theories given in this chapter and would more likely appear in the second year of 'A' level. In answering it, it is important to avoid too much description of conditions during the Depression; these are only incidental to what is required. You would need to consider the nature of the American economy and how the lack of regulation meant there were few mechanisms to put it right. The theories concentrate on what was wrong with the economy and why the conditions which may have helped recovery – government intervention through job creation and public works, for example – were not available.

## Source-based questions on Chapter 5

### 1. Unemployment

Study the extract by Dr Martin Bickham on pages 71–72 and the photograph on page 73. Answer the questions that follow.

**a)** How does the source by Dr Bickham show that men were willing to work? *(3 marks)*
**b)** Dr Bickham gave this evidence many years after the event. What are the problems of assessing the reliability of evidence of this description? *(4 marks)*

c) From your own knowledge, what sort of work do you think might be on offer on programmes such as these? *(3 marks)*

d) Dr Bickham specifically mentions 'man' and 'men'. There are no women in the photograph. Why is this? *(5 marks)*

e) How useful are captions on photographs? What are the advantages and disadvantages of them to historians using photographs as evidence? *(5 marks)*

## 2. Hoboes

Study the extract by Louis Banks on page 74. Answer the questions that follow.

a) According to this extract, in what ways were hoboes given a hard time? *(5 marks)*

b) How far does the information in this source agree or disagree with that given by Dr Bickham? *(7 marks)*

c) In the first two paragraphs, how does this source make clear the sense of camaraderie between hoboes? Give examples to support your answer. *(5 marks)*

## 3. Herbert Hoover

Study the parody of Psalm 23 on page 78. Answer the questions that follow.

a) How useful is this source as historical evidence of how Hoover was viewed by the American public? *(5 marks)*

b) What is meant by the line 'He leadeth me in the path of destruction for the party's sake' (lines 2–3)? *(2 marks)*

c) From your own knowledge, how fair is this parody to Hoover and his attempts to fight the Depression? Support your answer with evidence. *(8 marks)*

## 4. Roosevelt

Study the source by Franklin D. Roosevelt on page 86. Answer the following questions.

a) What is Roosevelt actually promising in this extract? Refer to the text in your answer. *(4 marks)*

b) Roosevelt is trying to bind the American people together in a common goal. Give examples of how he uses language to get this across. *(6 marks)*

# 6 Roosevelt and the New Deal (1): The First New Deal 1933–4

## POINTS TO CONSIDER

As you read through this chapter, you should consider the following issues: what was the purpose of the first New Deal; how far did the measures solve the problems they were meant to address; what were the alternatives to the New Deal; and was the first New Deal a coherent programme of reform or merely a series of measures intended to address different crises as and when they occurred? Many of the problems with the legislation did not fully emerge until Roosevelt's second, more troubled administration and these will be considered more fully in Chapter 7. For this reason you should think of Chapters 6 and 7 as two parts of one whole; only when you are fully conversant with the contents of both will you be able to consider the New Deal in its entirety.

## KEY DATES

**1933**  Presidency of Franklin D. Roosevelt.
Emergency Banking Relief Act.
Beer Act – abolition of prohibition.
Glass-Steagall Act – imposed new banking regulations.
Truth-in-Securities Act – regulated stockbrokers' practices.
Agricultural Adjustment Act – government help to agriculture.
National Industrial Recovery Act.
National Recovery Administration.
Public Works Administration.
Tennessee Valley Administration.
Civilian Conservation Corps.
Federal Emergency Relief Act – grants to states to help the unemployed.
Civil Works Administration.
Home Owners Refinancing Corporation.

**1934**  Silver Purchase Act.
Indian Reorganisation Act – Native American tribes reorganised into self-governing bodies.
Federal Housing Administration – to encourage home ownership.

# 1 Introduction

| KEY ISSUE What was significant about the New Deal? |
| --- |

## a) Significance of the New Deal

Two weeks before his inauguration on 4 March 1933, Franklin Delano Roosevelt addressed a gathering of American Legionnaires in Miami, Florida. Joseph Zangara, a bricklayer of Italian extraction, fired five bullets at him from close range. All missed their target, but Mayor Cermack of Chicago, who was with Roosevelt, was killed. Zangara opposed capitalism and sought to kill the man pledged to save it – and Roosevelt did go on to save the capitalist system in the USA.

His New Deal may by no means have been a cohesive programme – indeed, it often seemed contradictory. It may even be a misnomer to call it a programme at all. Possibly, it might best be seen as a series of measures to deal with specific crises, with little overall plan. Certainly, it is most easily categorised with the hindsight of history. Historians can look back to discern common strands running through the legislation and its implementation; they can see where it led and how its ideas were later developed. There is little doubt that at the end of New Deal legislation, the USA was changed forever and the role of government greatly enhanced. However, whether this was intentional is a point for debate.

## b) Roosevelt's Inauguration

The year 1933 saw the final 'lame duck' presidency lasting between the November election and the March inauguration. Following the passing of the 20th Amendment, the incoming President was in future to be inaugurated on 20 January. The four-month period of waiting to take office must have been particularly frustrating for Roosevelt. The Depression worsened considerably, with the outgoing President, Hoover, unable to introduce new measures to combat it. Hoover did seek to involve Roosevelt in a smooth transition and to agree on common policies. However, Roosevelt was non-committal to his overtures. He wanted neither to be associated with Hoover, whose credibility was shattered, nor to tie himself to shared policies with political opponents. Later Hoover was to accuse Roosevelt of stealing his policies and taking credit for them – indeed it was said that Roosevelt wanted the Depression to get worse so he could take credit for launching a rescue operation after his inauguration. Hoover could then be accused of having done nothing to halt the Depression. It is unlikely that there was any truth to these accusations. However, what is clear is that there was little difference at first between the policies of Roosevelt and Hoover. The big difference was in the men themselves and public attitudes towards them. Roosevelt came across as dynamic, charismatic and someone in whom people were ready to have faith. Hoover as we have seen, was tired, jaded and dull by comparison. There was tremendous expectation and excitement about Roosevelt's presidency; people were willing it to be something special. Certainly no incoming President had, since the time of the Civil War, faced so many problems. Roosevelt's inaugural speech seemed to offer everything that people wanted to hear – but ask yourself as you read it what it actually offered that was specific. 'The only thing we have to fear,' Roosevelt said, 'is fear itself.' He called for 'action and action now'.

1 Our greatest primary task is to put people to work. This is no unsolvable problem if we face it wisely and courageously.

  It can be accomplished in part by direct recruiting by the government itself, treating the task as we would treat the emergency of war, but at
5 the same time, through this employment, accomplishing greatly needed projects to stimulate our use of natural resources.

  Hand in hand with this, we must frankly recognise the overbalance of population in our industrial centres and, by engaging on a national scale in the redistribution endeavor to provide a better use of the land
10 for those best fitted for the land.

  The task can be helped by definite efforts to raise the values of agricultural products and with this the power to purchase the output of our cities.

  It can be helped by preventing realistically the tragedy of the grow-
15 ing loss, through foreclosure, of our small homes and our farms. It can be helped by insistence that the Federal, State and local governments act forthwith on the demand that their cost be drastically reduced quickly.

  Finally, in our progress toward a resumption of work we require
20 two safeguards against a return to the evils of the old order; there must be strict supervision of all banking and credits and investments; there must be an end to speculation with other people's money, and there must be provision for an adequate but sound currency.

To achieve these goals, Roosevelt would go on to ask Congress to grant him powers as great as those it would have afforded him had the USA been invaded by a foreign enemy. As far as the electorate went, there was no problem with this demand. The influential political journalist, Walter Lippmann wrote, 'The danger we have to fear is not that Congress will give Franklin D. Roosevelt too much power but that it will deny him the power he needs'. He need not have worried; Roosevelt called Congress into a special session which was to last for 100 days; these first hundred days of Roosevelt's presidency were possibly the most frenzied and energetic of any President with a considerable amount of emergency legislation being enacted and the setting up of many 'alphabet agencies' – new government agencies so-called because they became known by their initials – to tackle problems.

Cartoon of FDR throwing out Hoover's rubbish on taking office.

Indeed it may be no exaggeration to say that at the end of the hundred days, the USA was transformed.

## 2 Roosevelt's Presidential Style

> **KEY ISSUE** In what ways was Roosevelt's presidential style different to that of his predecessors?

One historian has claimed that the modern presidency begins with Roosevelt.[1] There is little doubt that the main reason for this is the extent of the New Deal in expanding the president's role and that of the state in the running of the USA. However, Roosevelt also brought a new style to the presidency. He exuded optimism and confidence and was able not only to put this across but to enable others to share it. At worst, as was written in one business journal a few weeks after Roosevelt's inauguration, 'The people aren't sure where they're going but anywhere seems better than where they've been.' Roosevelt's style differed from that of his predecessors in several ways.

## a) Use of the Media

### i) The Press Conference

Roosevelt was perhaps the first president to understand the power of the media. He developed the twice-weekly press conferences into apparently cosy chats. The writer John Dos Passos suggested that it was as if Roosevelt was sitting at a table talking to old friends. He got to know members of the press corps by name, he explained policies carefully and he invited questions. This contrasted with his predecessors, who had only accepted questions written out and presented in advance. Hoover's relationship with the press had been so frosty that he had been accused of using the secret service to investigate any leakage of information to the press.

The result of this new friendliness and 'openness' towards the press corps was that Roosevelt could get them on his side, could release information as and when he thought it necessary, forestall criticism – and effectively control much of the newspaper reporting about him.

### ii) Fireside Chats

Roosevelt was said to have 'the first great American radio voice'.[2] He spoke directly to the electorate on issues in 'fireside chats' that became so popular that those who didn't have a radio would visit with those who did to ensure they didn't miss the President. The mass media was still in its infancy. Until Calvin Coolidge went in for being photographed (page 26), few Americans had ever seen a picture of their President let alone heard his voice. Here the reassuring voice of Roosevelt in living rooms throughout the nation restored confidence and helped people believe that everything was going to be all right. After he told people over the radio to tell him their troubles, it took a staff of fifty to handle his mail which arrived by the truckload; one person had been employed to deal with Herbert Hoover's.

## b) Appointment of Personnel

Previously Presidents had tended to appoint political cronies or at best other members of their party to help them govern. Roosevelt tended to look for the best people for the job irrespective of political affiliations. Most of the 'Brains Trusters' (page 85) followed him to the White House. In addition he appointed Henry A. Wallace, a farming expert, as Secretary for Agriculture; his father had held the same post in Warren Harding's cabinet. Harold Ickes, a former Republican was to serve for twelve years as Secretary of the Interior, although he was always threatening to resign; his battles with Harry Hopkins over the running of rival 'alphabet agencies' were legendary (see page 125). Hopkins had done social work in New York before being appointed to run the state emergency relief administration while Roosevelt was governor. Although he was a hard drinking gambler, he nevertheless had a vision of a country where the state cared for all those in need[3] and this would put him in conflict with many more conservative members of the administration. But Roosevelt enjoyed rivalry and arguments among his appointees. He would listen to their disputes and then make up his own mind between them. Sometimes he used personal appointees to investigate issues, by-passing proper channels. Often when appointing people to office he made their job specifications deliberately ambiguous so their responsibilities would appear to overlap with others'. He knew this would make people more loyal as they asked him to intercede in disputes or sought his favour or support. In the words of Arthur Schlesinger Junior:

> 1  His favorite technique was to keep grants of authority incomplete, juris-
> dictions uncertain, charters overlapping. The result of this competitive
> theory of administration was often confusion and exasperation on the
> operating level; but no other method could so reliably insure that in a
> 5  large bureaucracy filled with ambitious men eager for power the
> decisions and the power to make them, would remain with the
> President.[4]

It worked. Roosevelt inspired tremendous loyalty. He could enthuse with a smile or small favour. As Harold Ickes said, no matter how jaded you were, you came out of a meeting with Roosevelt like 'a fighting cock'. His appointees would need their energy. The first hundred days of Roosevelt's administration set the scene for the transformation of the USA.

## 3  The First Hundred Days and the First New Deal

> **KEY ISSUES** What measures did Roosevelt pass in his first
> hundred days of office? How successful were they?

It is difficult in this section to isolate those measures that were strictly passed during the first hundred days of the administration because they were developed and added to at later dates. The legislation of the first hundred days was that passed between March and mid-June 1933, during the sitting of the 73rd Congress. However, historians speak of the first New Deal as taking place during the first two years of Roosevelt's presidency. It is argued that a second New Deal followed this in which the measures were more radical. The validity of this thesis will be discussed in Chapter 7.

## a) Banking and Finance

The most pressing concern was undoubtedly the collapse of the American banking system. By 1932 banks were closing at the rate of 40 per day. In October of that year, the Governor of Nevada, fearing the imminent collapse of an important banking chain, declared a bank holiday and closed every bank in the state. At midnight on 14 February 1933 the Governor of Michigan followed suit; all 550 banks were closed for eight days. By the time of Roosevelt's inauguration, banks were in fact closed in many states. One important effect of these closures was a flow of gold from the Federal Reserve and New York banks; this was both to support bank deposits elsewhere in the country and to meet the demands of panic-stricken foreign investors who wanted to remove their capital from the USA. Between January and the inauguration in March, the nation's gold reserves fell from $1.3 billion to $400 million. American banks had only $6 billion in cash to meet $41 billion worth of deposits. In the two days before the inauguration $500 million was withdrawn. The situation was so fraught that Washington hotels would not accept out-of-town cheques from inauguration guests.

### i) Banking

On 6 May Roosevelt closed all the banks in the country for four days to give treasury officials time to draft emergency legislation. The ensuing Emergency Banking Relief Act was passed by Congress after only 40 minutes' debate. All the measures it contained had already been considered by Hoover. However they had been rejected because he feared the panic that may have resulted from the closing of the banks. Roosevelt had no such fear. Although his action may have been unconstitutional, people were expecting him to act decisively and, while the banks were closed, they improvised using barter, foreign currencies and stamps as units of exchange.

The aim of the Emergency Banking Relief Act was simply to restore confidence in the American banking system. It gave the Treasury power to investigate all banks threatened with collapse. The Reconstruction Finance Corporation, which became in effect the largest bank in the world, was authorised to buy their stock to support them and to assume many of their debts. In the meantime, Roosevelt appeared on radio to give the first of his 'fireside chats', explaining to listeners, in language all could understand, the nature of the crisis and how they could help. The message on this occasion was simple; place your money in the bank rather than under your mattress. It worked. Solvent banks were allowed to reopen and others were reorganised by government officials to put them on a sounder footing. By the beginning of April $1 billion in currency had been returned to bank deposits and the crisis was over. Raymond Moley, one of the 'brains trusters' referred to in Chapter 5, felt that 'American capitalism was saved in eight days'.

Roosevelt later drew up legislation to put the banking system on a sounder long-term footing. The Glass–Steagall Act of 1933 prohibited commercial banks from involvement in investment banking which had fuelled some of the 1920s' speculation; bank officials were not to be allowed to take personal loans from their own banks; authority over open-market operations such as buying and selling government securities was transferred from the Federal Reserve Banks to the Federal Reserve Board in Washington; and individual bank deposits were to be insured up to the figure of $2,500 with the insurance fund to be administered by a new agency, the Federal Deposit Insurance Corporation (FDIC).

The banking legislation, despite its success, was not without its critics, notably supporters of Hoover. They felt that all these measures could have been applied before the inauguration with their chief's blessing. On the other hand, some criticised Roosevelt for adopting Hoover's policies and for not being radical enough. Raymond Moley admitted, 'Most of the reforms that were put through might have been agreeable to Hoover, if he had the political power to put them over. They were all latent in Hoover's thinking, especially the bank rescue. The rescue was not done by Roosevelt – he signed the papers – but by Hoover leftovers in the Administration. They knew what to do.' While the Federal Reserve Board had been given more control, many critics nevertheless wanted to see more government control of banking possibly through nationalisation. Some felt that Roosevelt had even rewarded bankers for their past incompetence. Many banks had been given government subsidies to help them to stay in business. By requiring that state banks join the Federal Reserve system to qualify for insurance, large banks were given more control over smaller ones. It all seemed to favour the rich and powerful. However, what these critics failed to appreciate was the fact that this was precisely Roosevelt's intention. He saw his mandate as the saving of, rather than the destruction of, American capitalism.

## ii) Finance

Roosevelt saw his role in finance as primarily twofold: to stop the flow of gold out of the country and to increase the amount of money in circulation in the USA, thus raising prices.

In a series of measures taken in March and April 1933 he effectively took the USA off the gold standard by forbidding the export of gold except under licence from the Treasury and prohibiting the trading-in of currency for gold. Those holding gold were required to turn it in to the Federal Banks for $20.67 an ounce.

The main objective of these measures was to bring down the value of the dollar abroad. Once the dollar was no longer tied to the value of gold, it could find its own level in international markets. This meant in theory that foreigners could afford to buy more American goods. The measure did seem to work, because the international value of the dollar fell to $0.85 in gold, meaning that foreigners could buy 15 per cent more American goods than before for their money.

However, this success did leave Roosevelt in a dilemma abroad. European counties in particular had great hopes that the London Economic Conference, which convened on 6 July 1933, would solve their economic woes. Delegates from these countries wanted a general stabilisation of currencies. Roosevelt believed the falling value of the dollar was revitalising the American economy and so refused to make any agreement. This effectively scuppered the Conference and demonstrated how Roosevelt was concentrating on American recovery and how the New Deal was essentially a domestic programme. Assistance to help stabilise foreign economies was simply not on his agenda.

Moreover, Roosevelt wanted the dollar to fall even further than it had done by being left to find its own level. On 22 October 1933 he announced that the RFC would buy gold on government account above the market price which was then $31.36 an ounce. As the price of gold rose, the value of the dollar fell. On 30 January 1934 the Gold Reserve Act pegged the price of gold at $35 an ounce and the dollar had effectively been devalued by nearly 60 per cent (in March 1933 gold had been worth $20.67 an ounce).

At home, the effect of all this was to increase the amount of money in circulation. This, it was hoped, would raise prices; this was because in theory, as the volume of money rises, its relative value falls simply because there is more of it around; if the value of money falls, this means it will buy less, thus causing prices to rise. The rise in prices would in turn, it was hoped, help revitalise American industry and agriculture. However, while prices did rise somewhat it was going to take more than juggling the price of gold and currency mechanisms to effect any major economic recovery.

Roosevelt also sought to raise prices by introducing more silver into the coinage. He was persuaded in this by some of his supporters from silver-mining states such as Colorado. They had seen the value of silver fall to an all-time low and were looking for government help to improve this situation. Late in 1933 the federal government began to buy up all the silver produced domestically, at an artificially high price. The Silver Purchase Act of June 1934 stated that the Treasury would buy silver until the monetary value of its stocks equalled 33 per cent that of gold; or alternatively the market price of silver reached its monetary value. However, in effect this measure had little impact beyond subsidising the domestic silver industry. It offered a further lesson that prices could not be raised without real economic recovery.

## b) Regulation of the Stock Exchange

To ensure the excesses of the 1920s did not return two measures were passed:

i) The Truth-in-Securities Act, 1933, required brokers to offer clients realistic information about the securities they were selling.

ii) The Securities Act, 1934, set up a new agency, the Securities Exchange Commission, to oversee Stock Market activities and prevent fraudulent activities such as insider dealing. Roosevelt appointed Joseph Kennedy to head the Commission. Cynics held that, as a major speculator in the past, Kennedy knew of and could close all the loopholes! The appointment was highly successful despite the opposition of Wall Street insiders – some of whom had threatened to move the Exchange to Canada if the Act was passed. Wall Street gained a new credibility, and when the system caught and imprisoned Richard Whitney for embezzlement in 1938, it demonstrated it could now search out its own rotten apples.

## c) Economies in Government

Roosevelt was a conservative in financial matters and, like his predecessors, he believed strongly in a balanced budget. He was careful to differentiate between the budget for normal government business and that for emergency relief. He expected the former to balance. He sought to make all his recovery programmes self-financing and often they began with loans rather than grants. The Economy Act, 1933, meanwhile, slashed government salaries and cut ex-soldiers' pensions. Roosevelt also, like Hoover, refused to advance the veterans' bonus. However, when a second 'Bonus Army' arrived in Washington, Roosevelt greeted them with refreshments and entertainment. His wife was dispatched to assuage them and, this time, they departed peacefully.

## d) Agriculture

Agricultural recovery was given a higher priority than industrial recovery. This was for a variety of reasons:

i) 30 per cent of the labour force worked in agriculture. Increases in agricultural workers' purchasing power would, it was hoped, stimulate industry and put an end to the foreclosures which were, as we have seen, benefiting no one.

ii) The farming lobby in Washington had always been powerful. Democratic politicians representing agricultural interests in the South and West had been among Roosevelt's earliest political supporters and he certainly felt he owed them something.

iii) Roosevelt took a personal interest in agriculture. He regarded the farmer as the backbone of the USA. Given his wealth and political experience, this is an aspect of Roosevelt's thinking that is often forgotten. He remained passionately concerned with conservation and ecology, as illustrated by his personal interest in the work of the Civilian Conservation Corps.

iv) The increasingly militant Farmers' Holiday Association in the Midwest was threatening farm strikes if effective legislation was not forthcoming. The same organisation had disrupted foreclosures and both threatened and carried out acts of violence against officials trying to implement them.

In the long run, the aim of agricultural policies was to make farming more efficient by eradicating overproduction. This would be done by taking the most uneconomic land out of production and resettling displaced agricultural workers. However, in the short term, crises had to be addressed:

## i) Extension of Farm Credit

The Farm Credit Act of March 1933 brought all the various agencies dealing with agricultural credit into one body, the Farm Credit Administration. Next month, the Emergency Farm Mortgage Act loaned funds to farmers in danger of losing their properties. The Frazier-Lemke Farm Mortgage Act of June went a stage further. It lent money to farmers whose lands had already been foreclosed so they could recover them; interest was set at only 1 per cent.

## ii) Agriculture Adjustment Act, May 1933

Overproduction had been the greatest problem of American agriculture and neither the McNary-Haugen proposals of the 1920s nor Hoover's Federal Farm Board had addressed this problem. While industrial production had declined by 42 per cent in the years 1929 to 1933, that of agriculture had fallen by only 6 per cent. It was extremely difficult to tell farmers to cut back their production. If the cutbacks were to be voluntary, one farmer would be very unlikely to make the first move to do so in case none of his neighbours followed suit; if compulsory, there would need to be new and far-reaching enforcement agencies set up. Nevertheless, the main principle behind the Agricultural Adjustment Act was that the government would subsidise farmers to voluntarily reduce their acreage and production. The overall aim was to increase farmers' incomes to parity, or the current equivalent of those they had enjoyed in the so-called 'golden age' of agriculture in the period 1900 to 1914. A new agency was set up, the Agricultural Adjustment Administration (AAA), which agreed to pay farmers to reduce their production of 'staple' items – initially corn, cotton, milk, pigs, rice, tobacco and wheat. The programme was to be self-financing through a tax placed on companies which processed food. It was assumed that these companies would in turn pass on the increased cost to the consumer.

Reduction of cotton was perhaps the most pressing need. At the beginning of 1933 unsold cotton in the USA already exceeded the total average annual world consumption of American cotton. Moreover, farmers had planted 400,000 acres more than in 1932. They were, quite simply, paid to destroy much of this. A total of 10.5 million acres were ploughed under, and the price of cotton accordingly rose from 6.5 cents per pound in 1932 to 10 cents in 1933. However, it was one thing to destroy cotton but it was far more contentious to destroy food when so many Americans were hungry. Six million piglets were bought and slaughtered. Although many of the carcasses were subsequently processed and fed to the unemployed, the public outcry was enormous. In fact, only cotton and piglets were destroyed by the AAA. Drought helped to make the 1933 wheat crop the poorest since 1896, and agreements were reached to limit acreage in other crops in subsequent years. In 1933, 10.4 million acres were removed from production, in 1934, 35.7 million acres and in 1935, 30.3 million acres. Total farm income rose from $4.5 billion in 1932 to $6.9 billion in 1935. The percentage of farmers signing up for AAA agreements was high at first – 95 per cent of tobacco growers, for example – and the Act was very popular with farmers.

Faced by drought, western ranchers sought to bring beef cattle under the protection of the AAA in 1934. By January 1935 the government had purchased 8.3 million head of cattle, in return for which ranchers agreed to reduce breeding cows by 20 per cent in 1937. Overall, it would appear that the AAA worked effectively to deal with the crisis of overproduction, although there were problems which will be considered in Chapter 7.

### iii) Tennessee Valley Authority, May 1933

One of the most grandiose schemes of the New Deal, the Tennessee Valley Authority (TVA), was created to harness the power of the River Tennessee which ran through seven of the poorest states in the USA. It was hoped that by doing this prosperity would be promoted in a region of 80,000 square miles with a population of 2 million. The TVA was to construct 20 huge dams to control the floods which so beset the region; to develop ecological schemes such as tree planting to stop soil erosion; to encourage farmers to use more efficient means of cultivation such as contour ploughing; to provide jobs by setting up fertiliser manufacture factories; to develop welfare and educational programmes; and, most significantly perhaps, as a by-product of the work of the dams, to produce hydro-electric power for an area whose existing supplies of electricity were limited to two out of every 100 farms. The designers of the TVA deliberately stated in the Act that the production of electricity was only a by-product. This was because they knew private concerns would oppose the right of a government agency to manufacture and sell electricity even though they had themselves largely by-passed the region concerned. The electricity generated was moreover cheaper than elsewhere. The TVA effectively became a central planning authority for the region and was largely responsible for the modernisation and improved living standards that saw its residents increase their average income by 200 per cent in the period 1929 to 1949.

## e) Industrial Recovery

The promotion of industrial recovery was a priority for the New Deal. However, it had only limited success in doing this. Partly this was due to the scale of the industrial collapse. This meant that, although the economy grew 10 per cent per annum during Roosevelt's first term, output had fallen so low since 1929 that this still left unemployment at 14 per cent.

Roosevelt's primary aims were to put people to work and to increase purchasing power so consumers could buy more. To do this, he needed both to act quickly before the situation got even worse and to gain the participatory support of businessmen. He knew he could achieve little without the latter; there was simply no alternative structure to effect reform without the active co-operation of businessmen. They would hardly consent to radical policies such as nationalisation or anti-trust legislation. Again, it is important to note that Roosevelt was in the business of saving the American system of capitalism not replacing it. This came as a disappointment to many who had hoped for more radical objectives – as can be illustrated by the following concerns evinced by Benjamin Stolberg and Warren Jay Vinton.

1  The thing that outrages our social economy is the irresistible power of great wealth. The ravages which Big Ownership inflicts upon our society can be gauged on the slide rule of economic statistics. The figures are clear. What is good for Big Ownership is bad for the rest of us. There
5  is an invariable correlation between the upward concentration of wealth and the progressive crippling of our economy. Nothing can be really balanced in an economy in which more than half the national wealth is owned by less than half a million people, and controlled by a mere handful. In short, the interests of Big Ownership and the interests of the
10  American people are today completely opposed. They can be neither theoretically reconciled nor realistically compromised. ...
     No American President had ever received a clearer mandate to lead than did Mr. Roosevelt. He was elected to curb the irresponsible power of Big Ownership, to redress the unbalance between capital and labour,
15  to lift the curse of unemployment, to fight for a more just distribution of the national income. And so he understood his mandate, for these were his promises. The New Deal could do no less and be a New Deal. The New Deal could not get for the wage-earners a larger share of the national income without restricting the profits of Big Ownership. It
20  could not rehabilitate the American farmer without drastically reducing the tariff. It could not set up effective social insurance against unemployment, old age and sickness without making Big Ownership pay part

of the cost through income and inheritance taxation. The New Deal
could not reconcile the property interests which batten on restricted
25 production with the public interests which need productive abundance.
    But this is precisely what the New Deal has been trying to do all
along. Mr. Roosevelt has the kind of open mind which accepts with
equal hospitality the most contradictory views and the most irreconcil-
able facts. His whole policy is bent on ignoring the contradictions in our
30 economy. And by the very denial of these contradictions the New Deal
is forced to administer their contradictoriness, thereby deepening
them. It tries to make for a saner economy by strengthening all the
opposing forces of the status quo, thereby inevitably strengthening the
forces already in power.

There was no consensus about how to go about ensuring industrial
recovery.

Some still advocated policies of laissez-faire; others wanted massive
government intervention. Some felt competition should be eradi-
cated; others believed it to be the lynchpin of recovery. Roosevelt was
forced to act quickly and under pressure as Congress was about to
pass a measure to restrict the working week to 30 hours – it was hoped
this would necessitate the sharing out of jobs. Roosevelt opposed this
scheme because rather than raise overall purchasing power he feared
it would simply share out more thinly that which already existed. The
measure with which he replaced it was the National Industry Recovery
Act of June 1933. The Act came in two parts.

## i) National Recovery Administration

This was set up to oversee industrial recovery. Headed by General
Hugh Johnson, an irascible, hard-drinking dynamo of energy, it
seemed to offer something to all groups involved in industry.
Powerful businessmen, for example, benefited from anti-trust legislation being suspended for two years. The argument behind this was
that if industrial expansion was to be promoted, it was crazy to maintain laws that, in fact, restricted it. Employees were to have the right
to collective bargaining enshrined in federal law for the first time.
This would necessitate the recognition by employers of trade unions
to negotiate on behalf of their members. Firms were encouraged to
agree to codes of practice to regulate unfair competition such as price
cutting, and to agree on such matters as working conditions and minimum wages in their industry. However, problems with most of the
operations of NIRA soon manifested themselves.

Many of the codes, for example, turned out to be either largely
symbolic, exploitative or downright unworkable. This was in part
because they were adopted so quickly, often without proper thought
or planning. They began with a great fanfare. A hectic promotional
campaign took place to promote the NRA and the codes. At a mam-
moth NRA parade in New York, for example, the singer Al Jolson

enthused before the newsreel cameras that this was the most exciting day of his life, more exciting, in fact, than the day of his own wedding! The national response to the campaign was tremendous. Eventually, 557 codes were drawn up covering most industries, and firms which agreed to them were entitled to display what would become one of the most enduring symbols of the New Deal; a blue eagle, with the logo underneath, 'We do our part'. It was hoped that consumers would support those firms that bore the blue eagle and boycott those which did not. To hasten proceedings, Johnson had drawn up a blanket code known as the President's Re-employment Agreement. This was particularly intended for small firms to subscribe to in order to take advantage of the blue eagle and the increased custom it would presumably attract.

However, the codes were often contentious. Many large manufacturers, notably Henry Ford, never subscribed to them and yet as we shall see, small firms complained that they favoured big business. Many small firms found it difficult to comply with all their regulations, particularly the minimum wages clauses. It was hoped, for example, that the firms signing the codes would institute a minimum wage of $11 for a 40-hour week. Few small firms could afford this. In March 1934 Congress set up the National Recovery Review Board to investigate whether small firms were disadvantaged by the codes. It was reported that they were indeed placed at a severe disadvantage. Moreover, the codes seemed to favour large companies that could take advantage of them to restrict competition and increase their profits. They could, for example, work together to draw up codes in which they agreed to raise prices while keeping wages low. Some agreed to limit output to raise prices and could therefore afford to cut back on their workforce or pay lower wages. Ultimately, moreover, despite the fanfare, the codes did not help economic recovery. Because economic recovery was so disappointing, Johnson attempted a 'Buy Now' campaign in October 1933. He also advocated an overall 10 per cent wage increase and ten-hour cut in the working week. Neither was successful. In reality, the NRA codes might look impressive but they could not in themselves bring about an economic recovery. Many critics argued that, in practice, they did little except give large firms the opportunity to indulge in unfair practices – the very opposite of what they had been intended to do. Johnson, a successful businessman himself, believed very firmly in self-government by business. There were to be no new government powers of coercion. Indeed, as mentioned earlier, the government had agreed to suspend anti-trust legislation for two years. The argument that the NRA favoured big business was, in fact, a particularly persuasive argument. The codes, for example, were largely drawn up by representatives from big business, often with the assistance of inexperienced White House officials. One of the first tasks of one recently appointed young government official, for example, was to confer with sharp company lawyers to draw up the petroleum codes, even though he knew nothing about the industry. Moreover, as we have already seen, the codes could be used for restrictive practices, such as price fixing, by big business. It was also felt that there was too much bureaucracy attached to the codes. Much of their credibility was lost when a dry cleaner was sent to prison for charging less than the agreed code price for pressing a pair of trousers. There was even a code for striptease artistes that stipulated the number of performers in each show!

Elsewhere in the NRA legislation 'yellow dog' clauses, discussed in Chapter 2, were outlawed, and Section 7(a) declared employees had a right to join trade unions and participate in collective bargaining. Roosevelt had not welcomed this clause, which had been forced on him by Congress. He was more interested in reducing unemployment than legalising unions. His fears that this could lead to industrial unrest seemed vindicated by the wave of violent strikes which were to require further legislation to alleviate. Unions said Section 7(a) was too weak for their needs and that many employers, including those who did subscribe to the codes, were still riding roughshod over them. Ford, who did not subscribe to any codes, kept a gang of union bashers on the payroll. Johnson created labour advisory boards to mediate in disputes but because these were advisory, they had little influence. Moreover, Johnson had made many powerful enemies with his high-handed ways and the press made a field day not only of his drinking but also of the high salary he gave to his secretary, Frances Robinson, whom he admitted was 'more than a stenographer'. He began to be an embarrassment to the administration and had to go. Roosevelt dismissed him in September 1934. After his departure some of the codes were relaxed but, as we shall see in Chapter 7, the Supreme Court dealt the death blow in May 1935 when it declared the NRA unconstitutional.

## ii) Public Works Administration (PWA)

The second part of NIRA set up an emergency Public Works Administration to be headed by the Secretary of the Interior, Harold Ickes. It was funded with $3.3 billion and its purpose was 'pump priming'. It was hoped that expenditure on public works such as roads, dams, hospitals and schools would stimulate the economy. Ickes was a meticulous administrator who therefore made progress very slowly. In fact, he was criticised for spending only $110 million of his funding in the first six months. However, he demanded value for money and would only fund worthwhile projects. He did not want to have the agency jeopardised by criticisms that it was wasting taxpayers' money – or 'boondoggling' in popular parlance – a viewpoint fully endorsed by the President. Moreover, public works projects involve lengthy preparations with design, planning, submission of contracts and so on. Eventually the PWA put hundreds of thousands of people to work, building, among other things, nearly 13,000 schools and 50,000 miles of roads.

It pumped billions of dollars into the economy and was responsible for massive public works schemes, particularly in the West, where it enabled dams to be built to help irrigate former semi-desert land, electricity to be produced and four vast National Parks to be created.

## f) Relief

One major difference between Roosevelt and Hoover was the willingness of the former to involve the government in direct relief measures.

### i) Federal Emergency Relief Act, May 1933

This act established the Federal Emergency Relief Administration (FERA). It was given $500 million to be divided equally among the states to help provide for the unemployed. Half the money was to be granted to states for outright relief and, with the remainder, the government would pay each state $1 for every $3 it spent on relief. Roosevelt chose Harry Hopkins to run this programme. He had administered the relief programmes Roosevelt had instituted as Governor of New York. The act said that each state should set up a FERA office and organise relief programmes, raising the money through borrowing, tax rises or any other means. When some states such as Kentucky and Ohio refused to comply, Hopkins simply threatened to refuse to send them any federal monies. However, there were loopholes such as restrictions in states' constitutions as to executive and legislative powers. Moreover, many states were wedded to the idea of a balanced budget and found expenditure on relief anathema. It was still felt by many that to be needy was one's own fault and those requiring relief were treated abominably. One FERA worker reported that in Phoenix, Arizona, over 100 claimants were jammed into a small room in temperatures of over 100 degrees while an overflow were waiting in a nearby garage. In many places there could be interminable waits and delays, the long queues often guarded by hostile policemen, uncaring officials completing endless numbers of forms and then long delays before any kind of relief was forthcoming. The Governor of Oregon went as far as to advocate euthanasia for the needy and sick while the Governor of Georgia offered the unemployed a dose of caster oil. The bottom line was that they knew Hopkins could not refuse them funds as the only people who would suffer were those the funds were meant to help – the needy and unemployed themselves. One governor even boasted that he had cut relief spending but still received FERA funds. What FERA could do in the face of such opposition – its workers were refused office space in some states and in some cases, their case loads were numbered in thousands – was limited. Its funds were limited too. In 1935 it was paying about $25 per month to an average family on relief, while the average monthly minimum wage for subsistence was estimated at $100. However, although its effects were limited, it did set the important precedent of federal government giving direct funds for relief and the principle had been established for future administrations to develop.

### ii) Civilian Conservation Corps, March 1933

Unemployed young men between the ages of 17 and 24 (later 28) were recruited by the Department of Labor to work in the Civilian Conservation Corps (CCC) in national forests and parks and public lands. The Corps was organised along military lines, but its tasks were set out by the Departments of the Interior and Agriculture. At an estimated cost of $5,500 million in the first year, 250,000 recruits worked on reforestation, soil conservation and forestry management projects. Initially they served for nine months to give as many as possible the opportunity to join; they were paid $30 per month, of which $25 had to be sent home to their families. Among the first recruits were 2,500 of the second 'bonus army'; Roosevelt waived the age restrictions on their behalf. The CCC was originally set up for two years but Congress extended this for a further seven years in 1935, when its strength was increased to 500,000. In the period of its life, the CCC installed 65,100 miles of telephone lines in inaccessible areas, spent 4.1 million man hours fighting forest fires and planted 1.3 billion trees. The CCC gave countless young men a new self-respect and, particularly those from the cities, valuable experience of both comradeship and life in the 'great outdoors'; 100,000 of its recruits were also taught to read. However, as we will see this experience was primarily available to young *white* men and, of course, their time in the CCC was no guarantee that they would not return to the ranks of those on relief when it was over.

### iii) Civil Works Administration (CWA)

This agency was created in November 1933, with $400 million of the PWA's money, primarily to provide emergency relief to the unemployed during the hard winter of 1933-4. While it put four million people to work on public works projects, it was closed down in March when the winter was over. However, FERA agreed to fund more public works projects itself.

## g) Native Americans

The new Commissioner for the Bureau of Indian Affairs, John Collier, was determined to reverse government policy towards Native Americans. The current policy was based on the Dawes Severalty Act of 1887. This had as its lynchpin the twin notions of assimilation and allotment – that Native American culture should disappear and that

Native Americans should adopt 'mainstream' culture. To this end, for example, children were taught in Christian schools and forced to adopt Western dress. More significantly, the policy of allotment meant that the old tribal units were broken up and the reservations divided into family-sized farms of 160 acres. Surplus land was to be sold off. The destruction of Native American culture had often left the people listless and apathetic. Allotment had been a failure particularly for those Native Americans who were not farmers by tradition. Moreover, much of the land allocated to them was unsuitable for productive farming. In fact, of 138 million acres owned by Native Americans at the time of the Dawes Severalty Act, 90 million had fallen out of their hands by 1932. Many Native Americans lived in squalor and idleness. Often unscrupulous whites had swindled them out of their land or had acquired it at bargain prices. By 1926 a Department of the Interior inquiry found that the act had been a disaster for Native Americans and that the policy of allotment in particular should be reversed. However, it was not until 1934 that the Indian Reorganisation Act did away with it, along with all the terms of the Dawes Severalty Act. The new act recognised and encouraged Native American culture. Tribes were reorganised into self-governing bodies which could vote to adopt constitutions and have their own police and legal systems. They could control land sales on the reservations, while new tribal corporations were established to manage tribal resources. However, these measures in no way relieved Native American poverty and, indeed, 75 out of 245 tribes voted against them – including the largest group, the Navahos. This group opposed the act mainly to register their anger at having been forced to reduce the numbers of their sheep due to overgrazing. Moreover, there was concern that Collier did not really understand Native American needs. For example, he introduced the idea of voting by secret ballot both to see whether Native American tribal units were in favour of the act in the first place and to establish democracy in the newly reorganised reservations. However, many Native Americans saw democracy as an alien 'white' concept. They wished to continue their own traditional tribal councils in which people spoke their minds openly, not voted in secret. The policy of recognising Native American culture also came under attack from some quarters. Collier was accused of encouraging Native Americans to 'go back to the blanket'. It was argued that they needed assimilation to prosper in American society. Collier also seemed indifferent to Native American resistance to the efforts of big corporations to exploit natural resources on reservation land.

However, Collier did do his best to ensure Native Americans could take advantage of New Deal agencies such as the CCC and PWA. In addition, his work was important in affording a new respect for Native American culture even if the culture was often misunderstood. Having said this, one must remember that Native American poverty was so great that these measures for all their good intentions could at best have only a marginal effect. As New Deal programmes wound down in the 1940s, Native Americans began to set up pressure groups and increasingly became in charge of their own destinies.

## h) Housing

### i) Home Owners Refinancing Corporation, June 1933

This agency helped home owners in difficulties by offering new mortgages at low rates of interest over longer periods of time.

### ii) Federal Housing Administration (FHA)

This was established in June 1934 to offer federal insurance on low interest, long-term mortgages taken out by those buying new homes. Clearly, this was an attempt to stimulate the building industry. However, the loans were solely for newly purchased single family homes; they could not be used to renovate existing properties or for multi-owner ones. The FHA therefore did nothing to help the increasingly blighted inner cities. In fact, one of the agency's unanticipated effects was to encourage the movement to suburbs. And with 65 per cent of new houses costing over $4,000 it was estimated that less than 25 per cent of urban families could afford to take out any kind of mortgage on them. The act mainly benefited white, middle-class families. Increasingly, inner-city areas tended to be run down and left to poorer ethnic minorities who were forced to rent properties that were often becoming squalid.

Now that you have read about the measures passed during Roosevelt's first administration, it is time for you to consider their effectiveness. How far did they solve the problems they were addressing? What common features can you detect in those that seem to have been more successful? Can you think of any reasons why this may have been so?

## 4 Alternatives to the New Deal

> **KEY ISSUE** What groups and personalities opposed the New Deal and what alternatives did they offer?

The New Deal attracted much opposition – from the political right because it was too radical and from the political left because it was not radical enough. In this section the alternatives put forward by some of these opponents will be examined.

## a) Liberty Leaguers

Many of the wealthy, who had supported Roosevelt in the darkest days of the Depression as the saviour of capitalism, now turned against him when it seemed that capitalism had, in fact, been saved. The Liberty League was organised in April 1934 to promote private property and private enterprise unregulated by law. Increasingly, its members saw Roosevelt as a traitor to his class; some refused even to speak of him by name but used cruel jibes like, 'that cripple in the White House'. Some likened the New Deal to Communism in the USSR. There is even a suggestion that the far right planned a coup d'état against Roosevelt in 1934 and that this was foiled by the very General who had been asked to lead it.[5] The Liberty Leaguers attacked Roosevelt throughout the New Deal years and formed the basis of right-wing opposition to him.

But, at the time, Roosevelt was more concerned about threats from the left, particularly that their authors might join together to form a third party to challenge him in the next presidential election.

## b) End Poverty in California (EPIC)

The novelist Upton Sinclair came up with a scheme whereby the unemployed would be put to work in state-run co-operatives; they would be paid in currency which they could only spend in other co-operatives. For a time, Sinclair's ideas gained credibility and he won the Democratic nomination as state governor in the 1934 election. However, concerted opposition, particularly from the movie industry in Hollywood, ensured that he was soundly defeated by the Republican candidate. Nevertheless his many supporters remained and proved useful recruits for more serious alternative movements.

## c) Share Our Wealth

Senator Huey Long, nicknamed the 'Kingfish' had built a powerful political machine in the state of Louisiana. He had done much for his state, ordering massive public works programmes – over 3,000 miles of paved highways were built between 1928 and 1933, besides new public buildings and an airport at New Orleans – and ambitious adult literacy schemes. However, he did govern as a dictator and opponents were treated quite brutally by his bully boys. In February 1934 Long moved on to the national scene with his 'Share Our Wealth' scheme. He advocated that all private fortunes over $3 million should be confiscated and every family should be given enough money to buy a house, a car and a radio. There should also be old age pensions, minimum wages so that every family would be guaranteed $2,000 to $3,000 per year, and free college education for all suitable candidates.

Long's ideas proved very popular and 'Share Our Wealth' clubs grew to 27,431 in number, with 4.6 million members represented in every state. Long began to talk of joining forces with other radicals to form a third party to oppose Roosevelt in the 1936 presidential election. In 1935, Postmaster General James A. Farley took a secret poll to assess Long's popularity and was shocked to discover that up to 4 million people might vote for him in 1936. This could mean that Long might hold the balance of power in the election. The Lousiana Senator was, in fact, gunned down in September 1935. While there can be no credence given to the rumours circulated by his supporters that Roosevelt's hand was somehow behind the assassination, the President must nevertheless have breathed a sigh of relief at the news.

## d) Old Age Revolving Pensions Inc

Francis Townsend was a retired doctor who advocated old age pensions with a difference. Everyone over 60 years of age who received no salary for working, should be given $200 per month on the understanding that every cent of it was spent and none saved. The idea was that this would boost consumption and thereby production; it was hoped this would pull the USA out of the Depression. Moreover, by encouraging people to retire at 60 there would be more jobs for the young. Soon Townsend Clubs had 500,000 members and Congress was being lobbied to put the plan into operation. It was, of course, totally impractical; payments to recipients would have amounted to 50 per cent of national income and an army of bureaucrats would have been necessary to ensure pensioners were spending all their $200. Nevertheless the level of support showed the movement had to be taken seriously.

## e) Father Charles Coughlin

Charles Coughlin was a priest whose radio programme, 'The Golden Hour of the Little Flower' was enormously influential during the first half of the 1930s. It regularly commanded an audience of 30 to 40 million, and listeners contributed more than $5 million per year to his parish in Detroit. At first, Coughlin had supported Roosevelt, telling his audience, 'The New Deal is Christ's Deal'. However, he later felt that Roosevelt had not done enough to change the banking system – Coughlin believed that banks should be nationalised. He contradicted himself by arguing that the New Deal was both a communist conspiracy and a means by which Wall Street financiers could keep ordinary people enslaved. In 1934 Coughlin founded the National Union for Social Justice with the aim of monetary reform and redistribution of wealth. Roosevelt was afraid of Coughlin's influence, particularly when a possible alliance with Huey Long was mooted. Long was assassinated, of course, and Coughlin became increasingly anti-Semitic – he blamed Jews both for the New Deal and control of Wall Street. Inevitably, perhaps, he began to look with admiration to the European Fascist dictators and this, together with government-inspired attacks, led to Coughlin's influence declining as the decade wore on.

## f) Thunder on the Left

This is the name given to various political developments which are credited with moving Roosevelt and the New Deal further to the left in 1935 and 1936. Governor Floyd B. Olson of Minnesota, for example, led the Farmer–Labor party which proposed far-reaching economic reforms. It advocated the state take control of idle factories to put the unemployed to work, nationalisation of public utilities and a moratorium on farm mortgage foreclosures. However, the impetus died with Olson, who developed terminal cancer in 1936. Robert Lafollette, Jr. and his brother Philip founded a new Progressive Party which had the support of eastern intellectuals and called for collective bargaining, unemployment insurance and old age pensions.

Although with hindsight, we can see that these movements probably did not constitute a serious threat to Roosevelt, how do you think they seemed at the time? At best, from Roosevelt's point of view, their apparent popularity may have signified the level of support for more radical measures to combat the Depression than had hitherto been attempted. At worst, there was the possibility that millions of Americans were so frustrated with the established order that they were prepared to vote for radical or even revolutionary change. While few of Roosevelt's advisers seriously believed this, as we have seen, the prospect of a third party at the 1936 presidential election was daunting, not least because it might hold the balance of power. What do you think?

Roosevelt, meanwhile, had listened to the mood of the country. In the 1934 mid-term congressional elections, the Democrats had made gains in both houses, with 69 out of 96 seats in the Senate – the biggest Democratic majority to date. Roosevelt was preparing a second New Deal that was not only influenced by the demands of radical politicians but also by the increasing opposition of big business to his measures. It seemed, in other words, that Roosevelt was beginning to take sides.

## 5 The Coherence of the First New Deal

**KEY ISSUE** Was the first New Deal a planned and coherent programme or simply a series of unrelated measures to deal with specific problems?

The first New Deal transformed the USA. No government had previously been so energetic in peacetime; no government had taken so much upon itself. However, the main question to consider is whether the first New Deal was a coherent attempt to change the political, social and economic structure of the USA or whether it was simply an ad hoc series of measures taken to deal with crises as they arose.

It must be said from the outset that Roosevelt did employ some people who did have a radical vision, who did see, for example, a permanent need for the government to take responsibility for the running of the economy, for people's welfare and so on. No doubt the New Deal was their blueprint for action. However, these people were not of one mind; they did not constitute one radical cohort which was in agreement. They tended to offer different, often conflicting advice. Historians have distinguished four different schools of thought among prominent New Dealers.

## i) Conservatives

Conservatives included Roosevelt's Director of the Budget, Lewis Douglas. He believed in only limited government interference in the economy, such as a public works programme to reflate the economy, but at heart wanted to leave existing structures unaltered.

## ii) Inflationists

These tended to see inflation as a means of boosting the economy. They particularly advocated the use of silver as legal tender; they sought to reduce the gold content of the dollar. They were pleased when Roosevelt brought the USA off the gold standard, but this did not go far enough for them. They sought, as we have seen, to increase the amount of silver in circulation and to reduce that of gold because silver was cheaper than gold. This would, it was hoped, allow the value of money to fall and hence prices to rise. The policy was largely unsuccessful.

## iii) Progressives

This group tended to share the ideas of the Progressive movement of the early part of the century (see Chapter 1) and to seek in particular the break up of giant corporations. Their leaders included Louis Brandeis of the Supreme Court and 'brains-truster' Felix Frankfurter.

## iv) Economic Planners

These wanted the government to take a far more pro-active role in central planning. Some, for example General Johnson, wished to see a partnership between business and government, while others, such as Adolf Berle and Rexford Tugwell, wanted the government to take control. They opposed the idea of a balanced budget, believing the government should go into debt to bring about economic recovery.

In particular, they supported ambitious public works projects and increases in taxation.

As we have seen (page 97) Roosevelt had quite divergent thinkers among his advisers. He often treated them as rivals – which indeed they frequently were – asking them to prepare plans, listening to their arguments as to the relative merits of them, bouncing them off others, particularly those he thought would disagree with them, and then making up his own mind. Roosevelt, for all his geniality, was his own man and he played his cards close to his chest. Advisers who were with him for years often said they rarely knew what he was thinking.

It seems with hindsight fairly certain that Roosevelt himself had no radical blueprint for change during the early part of his administration. As we have seen, he was himself a fiscal conservative, believing in the importance, in an ideal world, of the balanced budget. Certainly, in the short term, he kept on some of Hoover's appointees such as Ogden Mills. He maintained and extended the role of the RFC which Hoover had created. He differentiated carefully between emergency measures and 'normal' government business. He would readily spend federal funds on the former. However, as far as the latter was concerned, he cut federal salaries and refused the veterans their bonus. The very fact that he saw his role in terms of this dichotomy between emergency measures and 'normal' government suggests that he responded to crises as they occurred, 'crises' requiring emergency measures to deal with them. Raymond Moley reported that 'he was improvising all the time. Hit or miss'. This view is substantiated by Frank Marcus, an economist who worked for Harry Hopkins: 'it was not a clearly thought out program. There was much improvisation'.

No intellectual himself, but susceptible to a variety of opinions, Roosevelt welcomed and would listen to advice. He encouraged people with radical ideas because even if he did not agree with them, they could be useful sounding boards. In this atmosphere of government improvisation and initiative, all sorts of people with ideas gravitated to Washington and it was undoubtedly an exciting time. Insiders spoke of the air of expectancy, the feeling that a wholly new era in government had begun. Economist Gardiner C. Means, who worked on various New Deal programmes, spoke for many when he said: 'There was no question in our minds that we were saving the country. A student of mine remembered how exciting it was to him. He worked in the Department of Labor. He said "Any idea I had, I put down on paper. I'd send it up and somebody would pay attention to it."' There were radical agencies, for example the TVA which acted as a central planning agency for a vast area. The government did involve itself in direct relief. Many millions of dollars were spent on public works schemes. However, one should not be swept away by all this. Even if Roosevelt had supported wholesale change – and we have seen in fact that he had very conservative views – he had no mandate for it. As discussed before, he saw his role as saving capitalism not replacing it with something new. In any event, neither the structures nor the personnel were available to effect major changes. Many of the measures we have discussed were based upon speed of implementation. They also needed the co-operation of businessmen, bankers, farmers and so on. Truly radical measures would probably have earned their hostility and would have been impossible to implement – indeed, they may well have been dragged through the courts as unconstitutional. To Secretary of Labor, Frances Perkins, the motivation behind the New Deal was clear cut and humane:

1    When Franklin Roosevelt and his administration began their work in Washington in March 1933, the New Deal was not a plan with form and content. It was a phrase which he had coined during the campaign, whose value was psychological. It made people feel better, and in that
5    terrible period of depression, they needed to feel better.

    As Roosevelt described it, the 'New Deal' meant that the forgotten man, the little man, the man nobody knew very much about, was going to be dealt better cards to play with. The idea was not specific; it was general, but it was potent. On Roosevelt's part it was truly and pro-
10   foundly felt. He understood that the suffering of the Depression had fallen with terrific impact on the people least able to bear it. He knew the rich had been hit hard too, but at least they had something left. But the little merchant, the small householder, the farmer who worked the soil by himself, the man who worked for wages – these people were
15   desperate. And Roosevelt saw them as principal citizens of the USA, numerically and in their importance to the maintenance of the ideals of American democracy. The idea was that all the political and practical forces of the community should and could be directed to making life better for ordinary people.

This was accepted by most of the dominant elements in the Democratic Party in 1933.

In the light of the evidence, therefore, many historians have argued that it seems best to regard the first New Deal as a series of measures in response to crises. There seems to have been no master plan or blueprint for societal change behind them, certainly on the part of the President. However, not all share this view. There is a case that the very weight and setting of precedents of New Deal legislation did act as a blueprint for societal change whatever the President may have wished. Never before, for example, had any government intervened to such an extent in the economy and society. Never before had people begun to look to the government for help to such an extent. Never before had there been such regulation. Never before had there been so many minds at work in Washington to effect change. Together these factors did, in fact, even if unintentionally, lead to significant changes in the role many citizens expected of the government. What do you think?

As it was, Roosevelt was building up both, on the one hand, a considerable body of opposition to the measures he had taken and, on the other, powerful pressure for more radical change. Increasingly, as problems with his measures emerged, he found himself beleaguered and it is to these more difficult times that we must turn in the next chapter.

## References

1   W. Leuchtenburg, *The FDR Years* (Columbia University Press, 1995) p. 1.
2   *Ibid.* p. 110.
3   A.J. Badger, *The New Deal* (Macmillan, 1989) p. 191.
4   In Leuchetenburg, *The FDR Years*, p. 23.
5   C. Cramer, 'An American Coup 'd'Etat', *History Today*, vol. 45, no. 11, November 1995, pp. 42–48.

**Summary diagram**
The First New Deal, 1933–4

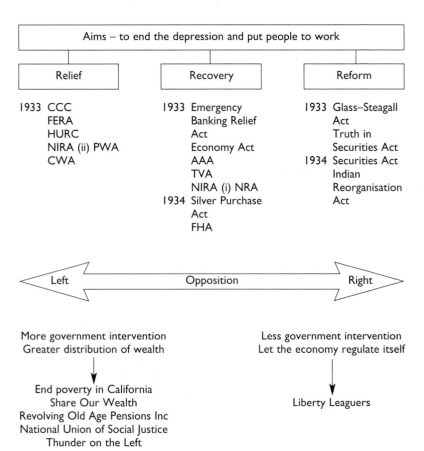

## Working on Chapter 6

This chapter has attempted to do four things:

**i)** To examine the purpose of the first New Deal (section 1).
**ii)** To examine the measures of the first New Deal in the context of the problems they were intended to solve (section 2).
**iii)** To look at alternatives from the political right and political left (section 3).
**iv)** To examine the issue of coherence in the first New Deal; whether it was a pre-planned programme of change or simply a series of measures attempting to deal with crises as and when they occurred (section 4).

When making notes, you should consider the significance and scope of the New Deal; describe the measures that were passed and also consider their successes and failures; look at the alternatives from the political left and right; and finally consider how far the first New Deal was a coherent package and how far simply a series of responses to different problems.

## Source-based questions on Chapter 6

### 1. Roosevelt's Inaugural Address

Read and study carefully the extract on page 94 and answer the following questions.

**a)** What measures did Roosevelt take in relation to each of the following statements:
  **i)** 'through this employment, accomplishing greatly needed projects to stimulate our use of natural resources' (lines 5–6); *(3 marks)*
  **ii)** 'definite efforts to raise the values of agricultural products' (lines 11–12); *(3 marks)*
  **iii)** 'there must be strict supervision of all banking and credits and investments' (lines 20–21). *(3 marks)*
**b)** Explain, using your own knowledge, how the policies outlined in the last paragraph (lines 19–23) were carried out. *(11 marks)*

### 2. FDR and Hoover Cartoon

Carefully study the cartoon on page 95 and answer the following questions.

**a)** Explain what message the artist who drew this cartoon is trying to get across. *(5 marks)*
**b)** Does the cartoon support Roosevelt or Hoover? Explain your answer carefully, using evidence from the cartoon. *(5 marks)*
**c)** How accurate a picture does the cartoon give of the political differences between Roosevelt and Hoover? Explain your answer carefully. *(5 marks)*

**d)** What is the value of cartoons such as this source to historians of the New Deal? *(5 marks)*

## 3. Criticism of the New Deal

Read and study carefully the source on pages 104-05. Answer the following questions.

**a)** What is meant by: **i)** 'Big Ownership'? *(2 marks)*, **ii)** 'the opposing forces of the status quo' (lines 32–3)? *(2 marks)*
**b)** Explain in your own words the argument of lines 1–15. *(6 marks)*
**c)** Is there any evidence in Roosevelt's inaugural speech to support the assertion, 'he was elected to curb the irresponsible power of Big Ownership' (lines 13–14). Explain your answer carefully. *(5 marks)*
**d)** Is this argument from the political left or the political right? Explain your answer carefully. *(5 marks)*

## 4. The Motivation behind the New Deal

Read and study the source on page 117. Answer the following questions.

**a)** What does the author see the New Deal as being about? *(5 marks)*
**b)** What does the author see as Roosevelt's mandate? *(3 marks)*
**c)** In what ways would Roosevelt's inaugural speech support or oppose what the author sees the New Deal as being about? Explain your answer carefully. *(6 marks)*
**d)** Is there anything in this extract to support the assertion of Stolberg and Vinton that the New Deal should restrict Big Ownership (page 104)? Explain your answer carefully.

# 7 Roosevelt and the New Deal (2): The New Deal 1935–9

## POINTS TO CONSIDER

In your reading of this chapter you should focus on: why there was a second new Deal and how successful it was; why Roosevelt won the 1936 presidential election; and what problems he faced in his second term of office and how successfully he addressed them.

## KEY DATES

**1935** Banking Act – regulated banking activities.
Revenue (Wealth) Act – increased taxation for the wealthy.
Emergency Relief Appropriation Act – set up WPA.
Resettlement Administration – encouraged farmers to move to more fertile areas.
National Labor Relations Act.
Rural Electrification Act.
Public Utility Holding Company Act – regulated the holding companies.
Social Security Act.
Supreme Court found NIRA unconstitutional.

**1936** Roosevelt's battle with the Supreme Court.

**1937** 'Roosevelt Recession'.
Bankhead-Jones Farm Tenancy Act – created the Farm Security Administration to help farmers in difficulties to keep their farms.

**1938** 2nd Agricultural Adjustment Act – established subsidies for farmers agreeing to quotas.
Wagner-Steagall National Housing Act – to clear slums and build more public housing.
Fair Labor Standards Act – fixed minimum wages and maximum hours for all firms engaged in interstate commerce.

**1939** Creation of Executive Office of the President.

## 1 Introduction

1 Dear Mr President,
This is just to tell you everything is all right now. The man you sent found our house all right and we went down the bank with him and the mortgage can go a while longer. You remember I wrote you about
5 losing the furniture too. Well, your man got it back for us. I never heard

of a President like you, Mr Roosevelt. Mrs — and I are old folks and
don't amount to much, but we are joined with those millions of others
in praying for you every night.
God bless you, Mr Roosevelt.

This is one of the thousands of letters Roosevelt received every day.
He insisted that his staff answer every one of them. There is no doubt
that many ordinary people regarded Roosevelt as their saviour. He
once said that everyone was against him except the electorate. He
never lost the support of the mass of the population and he was
regarded by many of them with something akin to love. People
believed he cared about and understood their problems.
Commenting on labour relations legislation – which, as we shall see,
Roosevelt rarely initiated personally – an employee is alleged to have
said that Mr Roosevelt 'is the first man in the White House to understand that my boss is a son of a bitch'. Certainly he was the first
President who spoke to the dispossessed, the have-nots in society.
Many historians have argued that the New Deal became more radical
in the years after 1935, that Roosevelt was genuinely trying to change
the face of the USA, that he was favouring the poorer classes at the
expense of the rich. They point in particular to the measures that
made up the second New Deal as evidence of this.

In the 1936 presidential election Roosevelt won a great victory. He
was at the pinnacle of his success. And yet, after this the New Deal was
beset with problems and according to some historians petered out in
1938 and 1939. It was ultimately, they argue, a failure because it did
not radically change the face of the USA. However, this can only be
considered a failure of the New Deal if it was actually an objective of
the New Deal.

## 2  The Second New Deal

> **KEY ISSUES**  Why was a second New Deal necessary, what
> measures did it include and what effects did they have?

When the 75th Congress met early in 1935 Roosevelt presented it with
a major legislative package, called by Walter Lippmann, 'the most
comprehensive programme of reform ever achieved in this country by
any administration'. There was considerable expectancy among the
White House staff. Harry Hopkins said, 'Boys, this is our hour. We've
got to get everything we want in the way of relief, social security and
minimum wages'. Eighty-eight days later most of Roosevelt's objectives had been achieved, and even some measures which he had not
particularly supported were also on the statute book.

Some historians, notably Arthur Schlesinger, Jr., have seen the
second New Deal very much as a change in direction. They see the

early New Deal as an attempt to reduce business competition in favour of greater co-operation through planning and government guidance. Clearly the NRA and AAA were examples of this in action. However, they believe the second New Deal saw a reintroduction of competition but with regulations about fair play as in the Public Utility Holding Company Act; fair representation for all sides in industry through the National Labor Relations Act; and a national system of benefits for those groups who could not participate in the system, through measures such as the Social Security Act. Nevertheless, as we will see, in attacking big business the New Deal's bark was always worse than its bite.

Before considering the legislation of the second New Deal, we need to examine in some detail the motivation behind it and the conditions which made it possible.

## a) Reasons for the Second New Deal

A variety of reasons behind the second New Deal have been offered by historians:

i) Roosevelt saw the need to respond to the radical forces described in the last chapter. It has been argued that, quite simply, he was politically astute enough to see the need to steal the thunder from people such as Huey Long, Francis Townsend and Charles Coughlin. He had no desire to see possibly millions of voters move away from mainstream politics in the USA.

ii) The mid-term congressional elections in 1934 had returned a more radical House of Representatives which was expecting legislative action and would support it. The Farmer–Labor Party (see page 114) could rely on possibly as many as 50 supporters in both houses. They were preparing their own programme that would have effected quite radical changes. For example, they spoke of maximum hours of work and minimum wages; greater investment in public works; higher taxes for the wealthy; and social security. Meanwhile, senators such as Lafollette and Wagner were also preparing their own independent measures. The climate in the new Congress was for action and Roosevelt wanted to pre-empt this. He did not, in other words, wish to surrender the initiative in preparing New Deal legislation.

iii) Roosevelt was increasingly frustrated by the Supreme Court which was beginning to overturn New Deal legislation; what he saw as their obduracy made him more radical in outlook. He also needed to introduce new measures to replace those such as the NRA which the Supreme Court had declared unconstitutional.

iv) Roosevelt was also increasingly frustrated with the wealthy and with the forces of big business who, as we have seen, opposed him more and more. He was particularly angry when the US Chamber of Commerce attacked his policies in May 1935. He believed he had been elected to save American business and he felt let down by its lack of continued support. Moreover, small businesses had benefited little from measures so far adopted. We have seen, for example, how many of the NRA codes discriminated against them. Increasingly New Deal employees in Washington were aware that small firms had a crucial role to play in economic recovery and many of the measures taken in the second New Deal, for example the Public Utility Holding Company Act, operated to their benefit.

v) Some historians have argued that Roosevelt was nailing his colours to the mast; that as the USA became more politically polarised, he sought the support of the left.

Each of these reasons contains elements of truth. As we have seen, many of Roosevelt's supporters were forecasting widespread support, particularly for Huey Long if he chose to run for President. The new Congress was preparing a programme of far-reaching reforms. It should not be forgotten that it was Congress that actually initiated legislation in the USA. However, increasingly the executive was telling it clearly what legislation it required. Roosevelt sought to retain the initiative in new legislation, to lead rather than to follow the legislature. He sought, in other words, to introduce his own measures for Congress to pass rather than to rubber stamp measures introduced in and passed by Congress. He had no desire to see a rash of measures initiated by Congress that were too radical for his liking. He was preparing to do battle with the Supreme Court which he increasingly saw as conservative and out of touch. We have already seen that members of big business – which Roosevelt still largely saw as the lynchpin of recovery – were organising opposition to him. However, one should not overestimate Roosevelt's apparent shift of focus. On 22 May he again vetoed the veterans' bonus payments and also called for financial responsibility in government. Many of the ideas encompassed in the second New Deal were not new to him, and indeed, he had considered several of them, such as old age pensions and the regulation of public utilities, as Governor of New York. New advisers did not necessarily herald a change in direction. As discussed on page 97 Roosevelt liked differences of opinion among his advisers and encouraged their rivalry. However, when it came to making decisions, he was his own man. Finally, there was no more coherence to the second New Deal than there had been to the first. Again, much of it emerged both in response to new and continuing crises and because the first New Deal had not brought about the economic recovery hoped for.

As we move on to consider the actual legislation, the following points should be borne in mind. We need to make judgements about how different it was from the what had been passed during the first New Deal and how far it was more of the same. We need to consider how radical it actually was. Finally, it is important to judge its effectiveness.

## b) Legislation

### i) Emergency Relief Appropriation Act, April 1935

This measure saw the authorisation of the largest appropriation for relief in the nation's history at that time – $5.5 billion – to set up new agencies to provide employment through federal works. There was some dispute between Harry Hopkins and Harold Ickes, both of whom vied for the responsibility of running the new agencies. Ickes sought economic recovery rather than simply relief and he wanted to see major public works that would aid recovery through massive demand for materials. He was, as we have seen, anxious that public works projects should be economically viable and value for money. Hopkins, on the other hand, wanted to put as many people as possible into productive work. His priority was to take people off the breadlines. While Ickes expected the actual projects themselves to aid recovery, Hopkins hoped the workers on them would effect recovery through their increased spending power. Ickes was only interested in projects that would make money; Hopkins was more concerned to put people to work. Given the high unemployment rate – excluding those on federal schemes, it was still 14 per cent in 1934 – Roosevelt favoured Hopkins' ideas and he was given control of the new Works Progress Administration (WPA).

The WPA recruited people for public works projects. It became a major employer. At any one time it had about 2 million employees and by 1941 20 per cent of the workforce had found employment with it. Wages were approximately $52 per month, which were greater than any relief but less that the going rate in industry. The WPA was not allowed to compete for contracts with private firms or to build private houses. However, it did build 1,000 airport landing fields, 8,000 schools and hospitals and 12,000 playgrounds. Although it was not supposed to engage in large-scale projects, it did so. Among other things it was responsible for cutting the Lincoln Tunnel, which connects Manhattan Island and New Jersey, and building Fort Knox, home of the USA's gold reserves, in Kentucky. Writers and photographers were employed to record American life, and art, culture and the theatre were encouraged through its auspices. The National Youth Administration (NYA) was set up to encourage education and to provide part-time jobs for students so they could complete their studies. The afro-caribbean educator, Mary McLeod Bethune, was placed at the head of the NYA's Division of Negro Affairs to make sure young afro-caribbeans got a fair chance. For example, she had her own fund specifically for afro-caribbean students, and she prodded state officials to make sure afro-caribbeans were signing up for programmes.

The agencies came under attack from all quarters. Conservatives predictably argued that WPA projects were of dubious value and that little real work was involved. In 1939 Congressman Martin Dies, chairman of the newly formed House Un-American Activities Committee, actually accused the WPA-sponsored Federal Theatre of being a Communist organisation. WPA writers countered these charges of useless work and left-wing political direction with the following song entitled 'Leaning on a Shovel':

1  When you look at things today
   Like the Boulder Dam and TVA
   And all those playgrounds where kids can play
   We did it – by leaning on a shovel
5  We didn't lift a finger
   To build the parks
   That you see in every city
   At home we always linger
   And read Karl Marx
10 If you don't believe us ask the Dies Committee
   Miles of roads and railways too,
   And schools and buildings bright and new
   Although it may seem odd to you,
   We did it by leaning on a shovel!

The writers' output was dismissed as crude propaganda for Roosevelt and a misuse of public funds. However, trade unionists were often fierce critics too, arguing that workers were exploited through cheap labour. Overall, most people agreed with Hopkins when he said, 'Give a man a dole and you save his body and destroy his spirit. Give him a job and pay him an assured wage and you save both the body and the spirit'. Moreover, the WPA employed people for only one year and did not compete with private enterprise. It employed no one who could have been employed elsewhere. Many of its projects such as surveying historic sites would not have been carried out by the private sector. In the south, some farmers bemoaned the fact that because of the WPA fieldhands and domestic servants were hard to find. If this, in fact, was the case, it suggests that they were exploiting their employees through low wages and poor working conditions rather than that the WPA was particulary generous.

## ii) Resettlement Administration, May 1935

It was decided to merge all rural rehabilitation projects into one new agency, the Resettlement Administration (RA). This was run by Rexford Tugwell who had grandiose plans to move 500,000 families from overworked land and resettle them in more promising surroundings elsewhere. This necessitated the purchase by the agency of good land, encouraging farmers to move to it and teaching them how to farm it effectively, using modern machinery and efficient techniques. He also envisaged the building of whole new 'greenbelt' communities. In the event, partly due to underfunding, only three were ever completed – Greenbelt, Maryland, Greenville, Ohio, and Greendale, Wisconsin. Rural problems were too great to be solved by the construction of three new towns. Overall, the agency only ever resettled 4,441 families and as such could not be judged a success. The reasons for its apparent failure were partly to do with the costs involved and partly the reluctance of people to move. While the 1930s were a restless age and, as we shall see, there were significant migrations, the strength of the ties people felt for their own home region should never be underestimated. Net migration from farms was less in the 1930s than in the 1920s. One of the main reasons why people move is not the promise of new communities but the lack of jobs in existing ones. With jobs in short supply everywhere, people tended to stay put despite the efforts of the RA. In addition, as we shall see, the government set up various schemes to help farmers remain on their land, leaving the RA somewhat at variance with policies elsewhere in the administration.

### iii) Wagner–Connery National Labor Relations Act, July 1935

Roosevelt was reluctant to become involved in labour relations legislation. There are many reason for this. In part he was simply uninterested in industrial relations. Certainly he had a very limited understanding of them. He was, it should be remembered, a country landowner at heart whose attitude to labour was more that of the benevolent squire than of the champion of the rights of collective bargaining. Moreover, Roosevelt was reluctant to become involved because there was a mistrust of trade unions in the USA, particularly among conservative politicians such as the southern Democrats whose support he needed. He had no more wish to become the champion of unions than further to alienate big business which generally loathed them. The act therefore was not initiated by Roosevelt. Indeed, he only approved it when it had passed through the Senate and looked likely to become law whatever his views. Nevertheless, the National Labor Relations Act is generally seen as an important part of the second New Deal and was a milestone in American labour relations. It emanated out of the disappointment with the Labor Board set up under Section 7(a) of the NRA. It was one thing to allow unionisation but quite another to get employers to accept it and the Board was generally felt to be powerless. The act guaranteed workers the rights to collective bargaining through unions of their own choice; they could choose their union through a secret ballot; and a new three-man National Labor Relations Board was set up to ensure fair play; employers were forbidden to resort to unfair practices such as discrimination against unionists. It was the first Act which effectively gave unions rights in law and in the long term committed federal government to an important labour relations role. However, as we shall see, Roosevelt still did not see it that way and preferred to continue to take a back seat in labour relations.

## iv) Rural Electrification Administration, May 1935

This act established the Rural Electrification Administration (REA) to build generating plants and power lines in rural areas. In 1936 only 12.6 per cent of farms had electricity, often because it was not economically viable for private companies to provide it to out-of-the-way areas. Where rural co-operatives were formed to develop electricity, banks were reluctant to lend them money because they could rarely afford the rates of interest. However, the REA offered loans at low rates of interest and farmers were encouraged to form co-operatives to lay on electricity. By 1941 35 per cent of farms had electricity; 773 systems, with 348,000 miles of transmission lines, had been built in six years.

## v) Public Utility Holding Company Act, August 1935

The USA had seen many problems resulting from the existence of giant holding company structures (see page 32). Stock issues were often fraudulent or overvalued and Companies were frequently powerful enough to bribe legislators either to stop legislation that threatened them or to promote that which benefited them. Rates paid to investors were often excessive. Holding companies were built as pyramids. At the bottom were the actual companies providing the utility. Distribution and co-ordinating companies tended to be somewhere in the middle of the structure. Sitting at the apex there was often a company whose contribution to the structure was negligible. Despite this, the lions' share of the profits went to those companies at the top of the pyramids. The actual utilities at the bottom of the pyramid, whose services fuelled the structure, were often kept in penury. Nevertheless they had to charge excessive rates in order to survive themselves and to finance the rest of the pyramid.

The act was quite severe in its extent. It ordered the liquidation of all companies more than twice removed from the operating company (some of Samuel Insull's companies, it will be remembered, were more than 24 times removed from the operating company). This destroyed the pyramid structure referred to above. It did this by making all holding companies register with the Securities Exchange Commission which could decide their fate. Any company more than twice removed from the utility which could not justify its existence on the grounds of co-ordination of utilities or economic efficiency was to be eliminated by 1 January 1940. The SEC was also given control of all their financial transactions and stock issues. Despite furious lobbying from the companies concerned, the act became law. Although some holding companies did refuse to register until the Supreme Court upheld the act, within three years the great holding companies had been broken up. The act rid the capitalist system of the exploitation associated with these companies. Most commentators agree that by doing so the act's major effect was to strengthen the capitalist system rather than to weaken it as the lobbyists had claimed.

## vi) Social Security Act, August 1935

It has already been suggested (see page 72) that the provision made by states for social security was wholly inadequate. For example, only Wisconsin provided any form of unemployment benefit and this was to be paid by former employers as a disincentive to laying off their workers. Roosevelt had long been interested in a federal system of social security. However, what he came up with was both conservative and limited in its provision. Certainly it was not as generous as Townsend's ideas, the popularity of which both Roosevelt and many members of Congress were clearly concerned about. However, the Social Security Act was the first federal measure of direct help as a right and would be built upon in the future. The act provided for old age pensions to be funded by employer and employee contributions, and unemployment insurance to be paid for by payroll taxes levied on both employers and employees. While the pension scheme was a federal programme, it was anticipated that states would control unemployment insurance. The scheme was very complicated. Employers were encouraged to participate through an incentive of 90 per cent exemption from payroll tax if they contributed to the state unemployment scheme. Since employees would pay direct contributions through the payroll tax and employers would pass on their contributions in the form of increased prices for their products, it was assumed that people would largely pay for the benefits themselves. However, reduced net wages and increased prices were two of the reasons cited for the coming recession which will be discussed later. There was also much resentment that the wealthy were not made to contribute more to the scheme. However, despite what many might have wished, it should be remembered that Roosevelt was not really interested at this time in a redistribution of wealth. In the event, both measures were generally inadequate. Pensions would be paid at a minimum of $10 and a maximum $85 per month according to how great a contribution recipients had paid into the scheme while working. They were not to be paid until 1940 so everyone first receiving them had paid something in. Unemployment benefit was a maximum of $18 per week for 16 weeks only. Assistance programmes for the blind, disabled and families with dependent children were also set up by the act, but although states received the same amount per child from federal government, the amounts paid varied widely – in 1939 Massachusetts paid poor children $61 per month while Mississippi paid $8 per month. Those needing most help, such as agricultural workers, domestic servants and those working for small-scale employers, were actually excluded from the act. This was because it was felt employers could not afford to pay the contributions and it would in any event cost the Treasury too much to collect them. It was envisaged that these workers would be included in the schemes later, once the act had had time to embed itself. Health insurance was not included largely due to the opposition of the American Medical Association, which would not agree to any measure that limited its right to decide what fees to charge patients.

Although the Social Security Act had serious flaws, it should not be forgotten what a major break with American governmental tradition it actually was. Never before had there been a direct system of national benefits. It is important to stress that this was not relief. Roosevelt refused to allow general taxes to subsidise the system. It had to be self-financing. Recipients had to pay into the system. The pensions were not paid at a flat rate but according to how much had been paid in while the recipient was working. Unemployment benefits were low and for a very limited period. Many conservatives argued that even this was too much. It would destroy initiative. It would make people dependent on the state. It took powers away from individual states and concentrated them in Washington. Many states compensated for unemployment benefits by cutting back on other schemes of relief. They increased residence qualifications and they made means - tested benefits more stringent. However, despite the limitations and drawbacks, the act signified a massive break with the traditional role of federal government. It was also sending out a loud message that it cared about people. It was said that Roosevelt took more satisfaction in this measure than anything else he had achieved on the domestic front. Why do you think this was?

## vii) Banking Act, August 1935

This act was intended to give the federal government control of banking in the USA. The Governor of the Federal Reserve Board, Marriner Eccles, felt that Wall Street exercised too much power in national finance and sought to repeal the 1913 Federal Reserve Act which governed the American banking system (see page 42). He faced powerful opposition from bankers, and, in the event, the final act was a compromise. Each Federal Reserve Bank could elect its own head but that person had to be approved by the Federal Reserve Board. The decisions on reserve requirements and rediscount rates were also to be given to the Federal Reserve Board. All large banks seeking new federal deposit insurance were required to register with the Board and accept its jurisdiction. In these ways the control of banking was removed from private banking to central government and the centre of financial management shifted from New York to Washington.

## vii) Revenue (Wealth Tax) Act, 1935

This act was implemented to pay for New Deal reforms and was perceived by those affected by it to strike at the heart of wealth in the USA. The newspaper tycoon William Randolph Hearst called it the 'soak the successful' tax. However, Roosevelt's main aim was not to see any major redistribution of wealth but rather to reduce the need for government deficit spending. Quite simply, the government sought to raise more revenue through taxation and it seemed logical to do this by targeting those who could most afford it. Before this, it should be remembered, taxes for the rich had been minimal – those earning more than $16,000 per year paid on average less than $1,000 tax. The act, drafted by Treasury officials caused long and acrimonious debate. Many of their original proposals such as a federal inheritance tax were defeated. Legislation finally created a graduated tax on corporate income and an excessive profits tax on corporations. The maximum income tax on incomes of over $50,000 was increased from 59 per cent to 75 per cent.

In the event, the new taxes raised comparatively little: about $250 million. For example, the laws regulating taxes paid by corporations contained loopholes which clever lawyers could easily exploit. Only 1 per cent of the population earned more than $10,000 and so the increased income taxes raised comparatively little. However, if Roosevelt had taxed the middle classes more, as he was urged to do by more radical colleagues, he would have cut their spending power with the resultant adverse effect on economic recovery. While the act did little in itself, it did act as a precedent for higher taxes during the Second World War.

## c) Assessing the Second New Deal

The second New Deal saw an important expansion of the role of federal, state and local government. There was much that was new. The banking system was centralised. Some of the worst excesses of capitialism, such as the colossal power of the holding companies, were addressed. The attack on unfair competition helped small businesses. Trade unions were given a legal voice. The Social Security Act created the first national system of benefits, although individual states operated the parts they had control over very differently. There was also the further development of existing policies, as with the creation of the WPA to aid both relief and recovery. The REA helped the process of modernising the rural areas of the USA. However, not all of the legislation was particularly effective. The REA enjoyed only limited success. The Revenue Act of 1935 alienated people out of all proportion to its actual effect. Some historians have argued that the second New Deal differed from the first in that the first was primarily about relief and recovery from the Depression, while the second was about the creation of permanent reforms. Having now read about the measures, how far would you agree with this assessment?

However, whatever the merits of individual pieces of legislation, whatever the significance of the second New Deal in terms of its philosophy, it is important to note that the administration was seen to be acting, to be doing something. It was seen to be addressing issues and concerns. It continued, of course, to involve itself particularly in everyday issues that were important to those individuals whose concerns probably would previously have been ignored. It was for this reason that the administration could enter the 1936 presidential election with confidence.

# 3 The 1936 Presidential Election

> **KEY ISSUE** Why did Roosevelt win the 1936 presidential election?

All parties agreed that the 1936 presidential election would be significant. If the electorate endorsed Roosevelt for a second term, they would be endorsing the changes in the role of government he had made. The Democrats were confident. There was no doubt that Roosevelt would be reselected as candidate. The economy was improving. In 1936 the volume of industrial production was twice that of 1932 and the value of farm products had increased from $4 billion in 1932 to $7 billion in 1936. Unemployment, while still comparatively high, had fallen by 4 million if those on the various relief schemes are excluded from the unemployment figures. The Republicans were in some disarray. It was easy to attack them, to tar them with the brush of the Liberty Leaguers – after all they were objecting to having to pay for measures which benefited millions of ordinary people. In the event, the Republicans chose Alfred Landon, Governor of Kansas, to run against Roosevelt. While he was not associated with the vote-losing policies of Herbert Hoover, he was nevertheless rather dour and colourless. Henry Ford called him 'A Kansas Coolidge'. There was little doubt who would win. In July Roosevelt compared his critics to a 'nice old gentleman rescued from drowning in 1933 by a friend but who subsequently complains that although saved, his fine silk hat had been lost'. His opponents, in other words, were ungrateful; they were against him now only because they felt secure again after he had saved them from disaster.

One essential issue was the changed role of government. Roosevelt said, 'Government in a modern civilisation has certain inescapable obligations to its citizens among which are the protection of the family and the home, the establishment of a democracy of opportunity and to aid those overtaken by disaster'.

Following the assassination of Huey Long, the left formed the Union Party in which Coughlin and Townsend endorsed the candidacy of Congressman William 'Liberty Bill' Lemke of North Dakota. Lemke unfortunately had a glass eye, wore outrageous clothes and had a shrill, high-pitched voice. One commentator wrote that, 'he had the charisma of a deserted telephone booth'. His policies, according to Roosevelt, appealed to 10 to 15 per cent of the electorate at most. Egotistical leaders such as Coughlin found it difficult to work effectively with others and arguments abounded. More significantly perhaps, while there was undoubtedly considerable support for particular issues such as Townsend's scheme for pensions, this simply did not translate into a mass willingness to vote for overwhelming societal and economic change. Few Americans wanted to change the 'system', particularly when Roosevelt, steering a middle line, was so popular.

In the election Roosevelt was triumphant. With the smaller alternative parties barely raising a million votes between them, Roosevelt won 60.8 per cent of the popular vote to Landon's 36.5 per cent and carried all but two states, Vermont and Maine, which were memorably shown in a subsequent cartoon to be in the doghouse (see page 133). As ever, Roosevelt had offered little in the way of concrete promises in his election speeches but people expected much of him. In his inaugural address in 1937, for example, he made a famous speech, which did seem to promise much. 'In this nation, I see tens of millions of its citizens – a substantial part of the whole population – who at this very moment are denied the greater part of what the very lowest standards of today call the necessities of life ... I see one third of the nation ill housed, ill clad, ill nourished ... We are determined to make every American citizen the subject of his country's interest and concern. ... The test of our progress is not whether we add more to the abundance of those who have much; it is whether we provide enough for those who have too little'. The implication was clearly that these people would be Roosevelt's priority; but he actually said little about precisely what he was going to do for them.

Roosevelt had fought the election largely on his personality and the trust ordinary people had in him. He was certainly aided by the disarray of his opponents and the fact that the Republicans could not possibly gain support by attacking measures which had benefited so many. Perhaps his victory made him overconfident and even arrogant. However, during his second term problems multiplied until his presidency seemed at times almost moribund.

# 4 Problems in the Second Term

> **KEY ISSUE** What problems did Roosevelt face in his second term of office and how effectively did he address them?

## a) The Supreme Court

Given Roosevelt's flexible ideas on the workings of the constitution, it was perhaps inevitable that he would come into conflict with its guardian, the Supreme Court. Although he had not directly attacked the court during the election campaign, he was very concerned about its operations and felt it was in need of reform. Although the court had supported New Deal laws in the days of crisis, it had increasingly

Maine and Vermont in the doghouse

declared legislation unconstitutional as Roosevelt's first term of office came to an end. In the 140 years before 1935, the Supreme Court had found only about 60 federal laws unconstitutional; in the years 1935 and 1936, it found 11 to be so. Indeed, on one day, 'Black Monday', 27 May 1935, the Supreme Court found the Farm Mortgage Act unconstitutional; found that the removal of a Trade Commissioner which Roosevelt sought was the responsibility not of the President but of Congress; and through 'the sick chicken' case, found the NIRA to be unconstitutional. The latter was possibly the most serious decision and it galvanised Roosevelt into action. The case involved the Schechter Brothers, a firm of kosher butchers in New York who were selling chickens unfit for human consumption. Prosecuted by the NRA for breaking the codes, the Schechter Brothers appealed against the verdict to the Supreme Court. It decided that their prosecution should be a matter for the New York courts not the federal government, and the poultry code was declared illegal. In effect, the decision meant that federal government had no right to interfere in internal state issues. While recognising that the federal government had powers to intervene in inter-state commerce, the court found that it had none to do so in the internal commerce of states. Moreover, if the federal government could not prosecute individual firms for breaking the NIRA codes, it followed that all the codes themselves must be unconstitutional. This was because they were developed by federal government but affected individual firms in individual states. The argument went that the executive had acted unconstitutionally in giving itself the powers to implement the codes in the first place because it had not the authority to intervene in matters that should be dealt with by individual states. Given that the codes were at the heart of NIRA, it could not survive without them. More significantly, the ruling seemed to imply that the government had no powers to oversee nation-wide economic affairs except in so far as they affected inter-state commerce.

Roosevelt believed the justices on the Supreme Court were out of touch. Of the nine judges, none were his appointments. He increasingly saw the issue of the Supreme Court as one of unelected officials stifling the work of a democratically elected government, while members of the Supreme Court saw it as them using their legal authority to halt the spread of dictatorship. The scene was set for battle.

On 3 February 1936 Roosevelt presented the Judiciary Reform Bill to Congress. This proposed that the President could appoint a new justice whenever an incumbent, reaching the age of 70, failed to retire within six months. He could also appoint up to six new justices, increasing the possible total to 15. The measure had been drawn up in secret, although, ironically, the idea of forcibly retiring judges had first been proposed by one of the present members of the Supreme Court in 1913. Roosevelt gave as the reasoning behind his proposal that the Supreme Court could not keep up with the volume of work and more justices would help. However, everyone knew that it was really a proposal to pack the court with nominees who would favour New Deal legislation. In the event, the whole thing backfired. It was not a matter of the most elderly justices being the most conservative; in fact the oldest, Justice Brandeis was, at 79, the most liberal. Nor was the Court inefficient. Chief Justice Hughes could show that the Court was necessarily selective in the cases it considered and that, given the need for considerable discussion on each, a greater number of justices would make its work far more difficult. Roosevelt had stirred up a hornet's nest. Many congressmen feared he may start to retire them at 70 next. He had also greatly underestimated popular support and respect for the Court. In proposing this measure, Roosevelt was seen as a dictator, and in July the Senate rejected it by 70 votes to 20. However, it was not a total defeat for Roosevelt. The infirm Justice Van Devanter announced his retirement; and, recognising electoral and political realities, the Supreme Court had already begun to uphold legislation such as the National Labour Relations and the Social Security Acts – possibly, as one wag commented, because 'a switch in time saves nine'. As more justices retired, Roosevelt could appoint his supporters, such as Felix Frankfurter, to replace them, but he did not again attempt to reform the Court.

## b) Agriculture

Although the AAA was generally regarded as successful, various problems had emerged as time went on. At local level it was usually run by county committees which tended to be dominated by the most powerful landowners. If for example, they were paid to take land out of production, they thought little about turning out their sharecroppers or tenants despite the attempts of AAA officials to mediate. Particularly where the treatment of afro-caribbeans in the South was concerned, officials from Washington and others who came to help were regarded as interfering busybodies trying to destroy Southern ways. Where the displaced tried to organise themselves – as in Alabama where they formed the Alabama Sharecroppers' Union – they were met with officially condoned violence. Roosevelt was reluctant to intervene because he relied so much on the support of Southern Democrats. In addition, there was an increasing feeling that the AAA only really benefited the wealthy. While farm income doubled overall during the 1930s, it had only reached 80 per cent of parity (the 1900–14 figure) and the increase was only 40 per cent that of non-farmers. By and large, much of the agricultural sector remained depressed.

To add to the problem, there was a natural catastrophe taking place over much of rural America. Years of overploughing in the heartlands of the country had made much of the soil fine and dusty. This had been of little importance in years of heavy rain, but in dry years which were coupled with high winds, the topsoil literally blew away. There was a series of droughts in the early 1930s which one weather scientist described as 'the worst in the climatalogical history of the country'. Beginning in the eastern states, the drought headed west until by the winter of 1933–4 the snowfall in the Northern Rockies was only 33 per cent that of normal times and in the southern peaks there was barely a dusting. Accompanying high winds led to massive erosion; the topsoil blew away in great clouds. The Natural Resources Board estimated in 1934 that 35 million acres of previously arable land had been destroyed and the soil of a further 125 million acres was exhausted. One storm between 9 and 11 May 1934 saw an estimated 350 million tons of soil transplanted from the west of the country and deposited in the east. Chicago received four pounds of soil for every one of its citizens. The effects were horrendous. Day became night as whole landscapes were covered with swirling dust. Homes were buried and formerly arable land was exposed as bare rock. Thousands lost their farms and were forced to migrate. It has been estimated that the state of Oklahoma alone lost 440,000 people during the 1930s, while Kansas lost 227,000. Many left to try their luck in neighbouring states. Usually their quest was unsuccessful. The plains states had little large-scale industry. Unemployment stood at 39 per cent in Arkansas in 1933, and about 30 per cent in Missouri, Oklahoma and Texas. 220,000 migrated to California in search of work. The 'Golden State' was usually unwelcoming. We have already seen how the authorities patrolled their borders, sending migrants back. They also expelled many Mexican immigrants. Despite these efforts, the state still had a drifting population of 200,000 migrant agricultural labourers, 70,000 in the fertile San Joaquin Valley alone. Farmers there were still reeling from a series of strikes in 1933 and 1934 in which the Cannery and Agricultural Workers Industrial Union had successfully seen wages rise by as much as 100 per cent.[1] Farmers retaliated by forming their own organisation, the Associated Farmers of California, which worked with the authorities to break strikes and destroy the unions, often by violence. They often used 'Okies' – as the migrants from the plains were called, whatever their state of origin – as 'blackleg' labour. Certainly the migrants were desperate for work. They followed the harvests throughout the state, travelling as far as 500 miles per year. Normally, they lived in filthy, squalid roadside camps with no facilities and high infant mortality rates. In one county, as many as 50 'Okie' babies died of diarrhoea and enteritis during the harvest season. They were often condemned as dirty and almost subhuman by the richer Californians. The state was extremely reluctant to help, seeing them as an unwanted burden. They looked to the federal government whose help also seemed unforthcoming.

To combat erosion, the government had set up the Soil Erosion Service in August 1933. This was later renamed the Soil Conservation Service and became part of the Department of Agriculture. It divided farms into soil conservation districts, and encouraged farmers to consider new ideas such as contour ploughing to hold the soil. Test farmers were used and evidence of their efforts were disseminated to promote the efficacy of their methods. The CCC planted trees and shelterbeds. However, all in all it was too little too late – and indeed if the land was reclaimed, farmers often began to overplough again and the dustbowl returned in the next generation.

When the rains finally did come, they would not stop. On 23 January 1937 the New York Times reported that floods across 12 states had made 150,000 people homeless. Nearly 4,000 were killed in the windstorms and floods. The problems were on such a scale that the government was unable to deal with them.

Although these events were disastrous in the short term, paradoxically in the long term they were beneficial for American agriculture. Many of the surplus workforce left and many of the remaining farms became bigger and more efficient. The Agricultural Bureau estimated that in 1933 about one in every ten farms changed hands and that about half of those sales were forced. This figure did not notably fall at any time during the 1930s. The human cost was incalculable, despite the fact that measures were taken to alleviate some of the misery during the latter years of the New Deal.

## c) Labour Relations

The mid-1930s was a time of difficult labour relations. Trade unions wanted to exercise the rights afforded them by Section 7(a) of NIRA and the Wagner Act, while many employers opposed them. At a time when many large-scale employers such as Henry Ford employed strong-arm men, strikes could often result in violence. There was also considerable anger at the use of 'blackleg' labour during disputes, particularly if the 'blacklegs' were of different ethnic group to the strikers.

There was, moreover, an important new development in American trade unionism. The AFL, the umbrella organisation representing American trade unionism, traditionally favoured craft unions and did not encourage the semi-skilled and unskilled to unionise. John Lewis, President of the United Mine Workers, in particular, wanted to see whole industry rather than small individual craft unions set up. If this happened it would be possible for any dispute to paralyse an entire industry. When the AFL continued to show little interest in this idea at its 1935 conference, Lewis and others who thought similarly broke away to form the Congress of Industrial Organisations. Later renamed the Committee of Industrial Organisations (CIO), this did encourage whole industry unions. Its first battle took place in Dayton, Ohio where rubber workers struck at the giant Goodyear plant. After the firm capitulated to the strikers' demands, the United Rubber Workers' Union became the first to affiliate itself to the CIO. A battle on a larger scale was to take place to gain union recognition in the automobile industry. At General Motors, there were 'sit-in' strikes for six weeks to gain employer recognition of the United Automobile Workers' Union (UAW). General Motors had produced 15,000 cars per week. During the strikes it was down to 150 and on 11 February 1936 the company recognised the UAW. Chrysler followed suit but Ford, using muscle men to beat up unionists, held out against the UAW until 1941.

Using the threat of massive strikes, the CIO had achieved union recognition in the automobile, steel, rubber, electricity, textile and farm implement industries by the end of 1937. Firms could not afford long drawn out strikes at a time of economic recovery. Union membership rose from 4 million in 1936 to 7 million in 1937. The number of strikes rose from 637 in 1930 to 2,172 in 1936 and 4,740 in 1937. Management was worried by this and the accompanying threat to its profits. The unions meanwhile were concerned about the level of violence used against them, which was often condoned and even perpetrated by the authorities. Both sides looked to Roosevelt for help, but he alienated each by doing nothing. He felt that the two sides had to solve the problems for themselves. He had never been especially sympathetic to trade unions; hardly any of the New Deal legislation supporting them had been initiated by him. Indeed, as we have seen, he had only given his support to the Wagner Act when it had already passed through the Senate. However, as the unions gained in power, Roosevelt could not continue to ignore them, and by 1940 they made the largest contribution to the Democratic Party's campaign funds and in return their leaders expected consultations at the highest levels.

## d) The 'Roosevelt Recession', 1937–8

Federal expenditure was cut in June 1937 to meet Roosevelt's long-held belief in a balanced budget. He hoped business had by this time recovered sufficiently to make good the contraction in the money supply caused by government cutbacks. It had not. The graph below shows how unemployment rose, particularly among farm workers in 1937/8. With the numbers of unemployed rising to 7.5 million in 11 months, social security payments swallowed $2 billion of the nation's wealth. The same problems of human misery that had been witnessed in the early years of the decade returned in full force. In the manufacturing industries, employment fell by 23 per cent and the production of such items as motor cars fell by as much as 50 per cent. Overall, national income fell by 13 per cent. Recovery suddenly seemed as far away as ever. According to the Federal Reserve Board's index of industrial production, 66 per cent of the gains made during the New Deal years were lost. The fall from 117 in August 1937 to 76 by May 1938 was in fact faster than at any time during the earlier depression of 1929 to 1933. Farm prices fell by 20 per cent. Big business was made a scapegoat for the collapse. A Temporary National Economic Committee (TNEC) was speedily set up to investigate price fixing among large corporations as many government officials thought these practices were responsible for the recession. In the event, the mass of evidence the Committee collected led to little in the way of government action because by the time it reported the recession was over. In any case, there was little political will to take on the giant corporations. While there was much popular sympathy for small companies and their difficulties, people increasingly realised the benefits of large ones with their relatively cheap, mass-produced goods that small companies could not provide. In this sense, the New Deal always supported big business, even though it often verbally attacked it. This perceived hostility led to a lack of morale among businessmen and accounts for their frequent opposition to the New Deal. However, we must remember that, despite his attacks, Roosevelt expected big business to lead the USA out of the recession. However it was ill disposed to do so because of the attacks. Representatives of big business in their turn blamed too much government and too high taxes for their problems. Many sought a return to the policies of the 1920s.

Meanwhile, Roosevelt seemed undecided in the face of the mounting economic problems. His Treasury Secretary, Henry Morgenthal, was advising him to balance the budget, while the chief of the Federal Reserve Board, Marriner Eccles, insisted that he return to deficit spending. In April 1938 Roosevelt finally chose the latter and asked

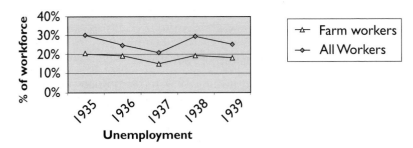

Unemployed as % of the Workforce

(figures taken from J. A. Garraty, *The American Nation*, vol. 2 (HarperCollins, 1999), p. 770)

Congress to vote him a $3.8 billion relief budget with the lion's share going to the PWA and WPA. However, recovery was slow and in 1939 unemployment still stood at 9 million. Roosevelt did appear to be moving towards Keynsian policies of massive government intervention in the economy and deficit spending, but his conversion was slow and reluctant. However, by the later 1930s he did seem to give more credence and support to those advisers such as Harry Hopkins and Frances Perkins who had advocated this, and conservative Democrats were increasingly frozen out. As the decade drew to a close, the European war began to dominate Roosevelt's policies. War contracts and the opening of markets unable to be met by the belligerents brought about recovery and concealed the failings of the New Deal.

## 5 The Later New Deal

> **KEY ISSUE** Was there a third New Deal and if so, were its measures more radical than those which had gone before?

Some commentators have spoken of a 'third New Deal' between 1937 and 1939. This, they argue, was characterised by Roosevelt adopting the Keynsian idea of permanent government spending to solve economic problems – in particular through his response to the 1937 recession. However, this argument may be too ambitious. It may imply a consistency where there was none. It could be counter-argued that the measures of the later New Deal were more piecemeal than ever. As it turned out, much of Roosevelt's programme failed to pass through an increasingly hostile Congress. The national mood was for retrenchment of government spending, not expansion. This naturally limited the scope of what was passed. When you have read this section, consider which interpretation you agree with.

We have seen above how the 'Roosevelt Recession' took his administration by surprise and he seemed uncharacteristically dilatory in addressing it. However, problems in getting legislation through were already appearing before this. There is broad agreement that Roosevelt's second administration was something of a disappointment. The increasing hostility of Congress compounded by the President's increasing concentration on foreign affairs have led some to argue that it ran out of steam. Certainly, Roosevelt was frustrated in many of his legislative requests. He wanted, for example, the encouragement of more privately built housing and the creation of seven more planning authorities on the lines of the TVA. Nothing came of either. As we will see, he went through with his plan to reorganise the executive in the face of congressional disapproval. This is not to suggest that pressing concerns were not addressed or that advances were not made. However, on the whole the legislation of Roosevelt's second administration seems nowhere near as comprehensive as that of his first.

## a) Agriculture

### i) Bankhead-Jones Farm Tenant Act, July 1937

This was passed partly in response to a report showing that as banks foreclosed, farm ownership was declining. The act created a Farm Security Administration (FSA) which replaced the RA. Its primary aim was to help tenants acquire low-interest loans to buy and restock their farms. The act was, of course, contrary to the RA which was intended to resettle farmers. The FSA was intended to redress some of the ill effects of the AAA mentioned in the preceding section and helped tens of thousands to stay on their land. It also established about 30 camps to provide temporary accommodation for displaced families.

The FSA also provided medical and dental centres and funded loans to enable owners of small farms to purchase heavy machinery. By 1947 40,000 farmers had bought their own farms through its efforts and 900,000 families had borrowed $800 million to rehabilitate their farms. Because of the return to prosperity as a result of the Second World War, the vast majority of the loans were repaid.

### ii) Second Agricultural Adjustment Act, February 1938

This was based on an 'ever normal' granary plan, storing surplus produce in good years for distribution in poor ones. It established that quotas in five staple crops – rice, tobacco, wheat, corn and cotton – could be imposed by a 66 per cent majority of farmers in a vote. Those who then adhered to the quotas received subsidies based on parity prices (those between 1900 to 1914). By concentrating on quotas the Act was meant to be fairer to small farmers than the first AAA which had given most subsidies to those with the most land. In case of overproduction, a Commodity Credit Corporation could make storage loans of up to 75 per cent of parity price. If, in other words, the market price fell below parity, the farmer could store his crop in return for a loan of 75 per cent (this was later increased to 85 per cent). When the price rose the farmer could repay the loan and sell the surplus. Moreover, the Food Stamp Plan allowed for farm surpluses to be distributed to people on relief – they would receive 50c worth of such commodities for every $1 spent on other groceries.

There were problems with this act. Its complexity left the county committees with so much to do they had little time to explain its provisions to individual farmers. As such, it was widely distrusted and believed to be unfair. This was particularly true for the small farmers it was designed to help. They had not time to study its details and had to rely on the county committees largely made up of the large-scale farmers they distrusted. It also appeared on the statute books too late for some farmers. They had already overproduced before they knew of the quotas for 1938. Farmers' resentment showed itself in the 1938 Congressional elections when Republicans and opponents of the New Deal made sizeable gains. The two politicians who introduced the measure into Congress were both defeated. However, having said this, the principles behind the Act – that of subsidies for farmers adhering to quotas – essentially remained in force until recent years.

## b) Wagner–Steagall National Housing Act, September 1937

This act was designed to meet the needs for slum clearance and the building of public housing. It was largely the brainchild of Senator Wagner. Roosevelt had little enthusiasm for the scheme because he could not comprehend the scale of the problem of housing in the cities and preferred to support home ownership schemes. The measure established the US Housing Authority (USHA) to act through the public housing bureaux in large cities to loan up to 100 per cent at low rates of interest to build new homes. Congress allocated $500 million, only half of what had been requested. The biggest problems lay in the great north-eastern cities. However, in a slight to them, it was stipulated that no more than 10 per cent of USHA could be spent in any one state. By 1941, 160,000 units had been built for slum dwellers at an average rent of $12 to $15 per month. However, this was wholly inadequate to meet the problem. It was a clear example of Congressmen from the West and South failing to agree to the needs of the northern cities. They increasingly saw these as getting the lion's share of the benefits of New Deal legislation. They were determined to reverse this trend. In addition, conservatives feared public housing was a threat to capitalism, driving away the private landlord. The result of the limitations of the Act was that millions of people remained in poor housing. It was only when urbanisation developed throughout the USA that Congress began to provide adequate means for public housing developments.

## c) Fair Labor Standards Act, June 1938

This act fixed minimum wages and maximum hours of work in all industries engaged in inter-state commerce. The minimum wage was 25c per hour, intended to rise eventually to 40c, and maximum hours were 44 per week, with the goal of falling to 40 within three years. The wages of 300,000 people were immediately increased and the hours of 1.3 million were reduced. The inter-state shipment of goods made by child labour under the age of 16 was forbidden and those under 18 years were forbidden to work in hazardous employment. To supervise the legislation, a Wages and Hours division was set up in the Department of Labor. This had the power to impose hefty fines on malefactors. However, to get the Act passed, particularly by southern politicians, Roosevelt had to make exemptions, notably domestic servants and farm labourers. As with the Social Security legislation, it was hoped that these would be included in the future – and yet, as they affected predominantly afro-caribbean occupations, the omissions could be construed as afro-caribbeans losing out yet again. It was another example of New Deal legislation bypassing them, an issue that will be more fully addressed in the final chapter.

Do you think the later New Deal was disappointing? If so, why?

# 6 The End of the New Deal

**KEY ISSUE** When and how did the New Deal come to a close?

In the mid-term elections of 1938 the Republicans doubled their seats in the House of Representatives and made gains also in the Senate. The tide was turning against Roosevelt. Although he was to break with tradition and stand for a historic third (and later a fourth) term of office, this was not known at the time. Increasingly as his second term drew to a close, he was seen as a 'lame duck' President whose New Deal policies had failed to deliver economic recovery to the extent hoped for. There were no new New Deal measures passed after January 1939. Increasingly thereafter foreign affairs began to dominate. However, one can discern a shift in Roosevelt's thinking. He increasingly realised that a balanced budget might not be possible in the modern world and that involvement in the economy and relief might have to become a permanent part of American government. This was quite different from his earlier ideas. In fact, some commentators have argued that when the USA was ready for radical change in 1933, Roosevelt adopted a conservative stance but when he tried to impose radical change during the later 1930s, the country was too conservative to accept it. In 1939, for example, opinion polls found that only 20 per cent of Americans were prepared to accept the idea of an unbalanced budget. Roosevelt faced three significant defeats during this period.

## a) Executive Office of the President

Recognising the permanency of the increased role of government, Roosevelt planned to accommodate this through the creation of the Executive Office of the President. This would lead to an expanded White House staff, a system of promotion by merit in the civil service, and development of more government departments. He was surprised by the general hostility to the idea. There was a fear that he was seeking to acquire too much power, that he wished to become a dictator, and that his appointees would use their new unelected positions to stay in power. Others felt that the President was trying to usurp the powers of the legislature which was supposed to initiate legislation. Some, of course, opposed it simply because it was promoted by Roosevelt. In any event, the House of Representatives rejected the measure in April 1938 by a vote of 204 to 196. Roosevelt, in fact, created the Executive Office by Executive Order in September 1939 as was his right. But it is important to note that this was with the disapproval of Congress.

## b) Revenue Act, 1938

In a further blow, Roosevelt's Revenue Act of 1938 was considerably weakened by the removal of the proposed tax on the undistributed profits of industry. Allowing firms to keep more of their revenue, would, it was hoped, help stimulate industrial recovery. Nevertheless, the message seemed to be that Roosevelt could not rely on the support of the legislature, that it was 'business as usual', and the mood was for lessening government involvement. In other words, Roosevelt had, in his increasing radicalism, gone beyond the mood of the politicians. More, the message from Congress suggested that the powers he had appropriated in the past were now going to be curbed.

## c) Roosevelt's Attempted Purge of the Democrats

When Roosevelt tried to purge his own party by getting rid of conservatives this also failed. In summer 1938 the mid-term primary elections for Democratic candidates to Congress took place. The President travelled the country endorsing liberal candidates and opposing conservative ones. However, the conservative candidates he opposed still made a show of publicly supporting him and in any event, these elections tended very much to be about local issues. Roosevelt's interventions had little effect either way but they did make the President seem ham-fisted. The attempt also made for difficult working relationships with the new Congress when it met.

Although each of these attempts to impose his will ended in defeat, collectively they made more people wary of Roosevelt's intentions. In August 1938 a Gallup Poll showed that 50 per cent of Americans feared dictatorship in the USA, compared with 37 per cent in a similar poll the previous October. With anxious eyes looking towards Europe and the growth of dictatorships, the tide seemed to have turned against Roosevelt and the expansion of American government. Moreover, Roosevelt was blamed for the recession, hence its sobriquet.

The editors of the New Republic gave a balanced assessment of Roosevelt's second term of office:

1   The New Deal, even in its second term, has clearly done more for the general welfare of the country and its citizens than any other administration in the previous history of the nation. Its relief for the under-privileged producers in city and country, though inadequate to the
5   need, has been indispensable. Without this relief an appalling amount of misery would have resulted, and a dangerous political upheaval might have occurred. Since the expenditure of money for relief – even the insufficient amounts recently appropriated – has been the principal target of the administration's conservative enemies, this accomplish-
10  ment alone would be sufficient reason for support of the New Deal. The assertion of the reactionaries that if the federal budget were balanced by cutting expenses, business would revive sharply enough to absorb the unemployed and make relief expenditures unnecessary, is incapable of proof and highly improbable . . .
15  All these extraordinary accomplishments must be remembered when we speak of the points at which the New Deal has been disappointing in its second phase. The most important of these is of course its failure to discover or to apply a genuine remedy for the stagnation of our economy, and for unemployment. These years have seen no
20  return to the conditions of 1932 or 1933, to be sure, but on the other hand no great or permanent improvement in national income, production or employment above the level already achieved in 1936. Nor have they seen the adoption of any important new means of bringing about such improvement. The President had apparently been hoping continu-
25  ally that business and investment would gain momentum of their own accord, while business spokesmen have been blaming what they call the hostile attitude of the New Deal for a lack of confidence which they charged with responsibility for retarding advance.

Roosevelt's personal popularity with the electorate was not in doubt. However, there was a feeling that the New Deal had run out of steam. In was in part Roosevelt's realisation that he had no successor in the Democratic Party who would continue his work that, along with the events in Europe, made him decide to stand for an unprecedented third term of office. As has already been stated, the European war and its effects in the USA overtook the New Deal and subsumed it. However, this should not blind us to its significance and it is to this that we will turn in the final chapter.

## References

1   A.J. Badger, *The New Deal* (Macmillan, 1989), p. 183.

## Summary diagram
Roosevelt and the New Deal 1935–9

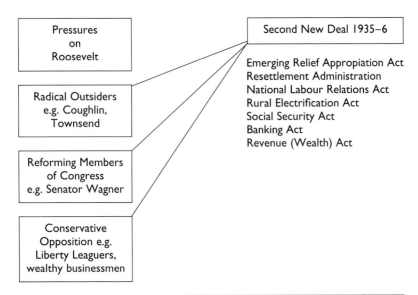

| Pressures on Roosevelt | | | |
| --- | --- | --- | --- |

| Radical Outsiders e.g. Coughlin, Townsend | | | |
| --- | --- | --- | --- |

| Reforming Members of Congress e.g. Senator Wagner | | | |
| --- | --- | --- | --- |

| Conservative Opposition e.g. Liberty Leaguers, wealthy businessmen | | | |
| --- | --- | --- | --- |

**Second New Deal 1935–6**

Emerging Relief Appropiation Act
Resettlement Administration
National Labour Relations Act
Rural Electrification Act
Social Security Act
Banking Act
Revenue (Wealth) Act

| Problems of 2nd term | How addressed | Level of success |
| --- | --- | --- |
| Supreme Court opposed New Deal legislation | Judicial Reform Bill | Bill rejected in Congress – but Supreme Court do begin to pass New Deal legislation |
| Agriculture 1 Working of AAA unfair to tenant farmers and sharecroppers<br><br>2 Dustbowl | 1 (a) AAA officials try to persuade local committees to act more fairly<br>1 (b) Second AAA<br><br>2 (a) Farm Tenant Act<br>2 (b) Farm Security Administration | 1 (a) Largely failed<br><br><br>1 (b) Mainly helped large farmers<br><br>2 (a) Partial success<br>2 (b) Partial success |
| Labour relations | (a) Did little to intervene in industrial disputes<br>(b) Fair Labor Standards Act | (a) Upset both sides<br>(b) Affected industries involved in interstate commerce but many sectors excluded |
| 'Roosevelt Recession' | $3.8 billion in relief | Inadequate to meet needs or to inflate the economy |

# Working on Chapter 7

This chapter has attempted to do three things:

**i)** To look at the reasons behind the second New Deal, and to assess the effectiveness of the measures passed (section 2).
**ii)** To examine the 1936 presidential election in terms of why Roosevelt won and what he had promised the electorate (section 3).
**iii)** To consider the problems during Roosevelt's second term of office and the ways in which he attempted to overcome them (sections 4 and 5).

When making your notes you should keep these issues very much in mind. You could draw up a chart:

New Deal 1935–9

| Problems | Solutions | How successful were they? |
|----------|-----------|---------------------------|
|          |           |                           |
|          |           |                           |

## Answering essay questions on Chapter 7

It is probable that at AS level you will get straightforward questions about specific aspects of the New Deal, such as:

**1.** Why was the Agricultural Adjustment Act passed and how did it benefit farmers?
**2.** Why was the National Industrial Recovery Act passed and why did many employers oppose it?

Clearly, to achieve a good mark you will need to address the specific issues raised. These questions reflect the need for careful and precise revision. You will get a little credit if you 'waffle' when answering them.

Essay questions often cover the entire period of the New Deal. Often they are concerned with how new a departure it was.

**3.** What was new about the New Deal?
**4.** How far did the New Deal signify a new direction in American policy?

To answer these questions you will need to consider three issues:

**i)** What sorts of areas and concerns did American government involve itself in before Roosevelt's first term of office?
**ii)** What areas and concerns did Roosevelt involve federal government in?
**iii)** How far was this a departure from existing practice?

Overall, Roosevelt expanded the role of government to deal with the crisis caused by the deepening depression. Many of his measures such as the Banking Act had been considered by his predecessor. Hoover had also given out more government help that any other President. Roosevelt could therefore be said to be developing a process which had already begun. You should also mention that in his early years as President, Roosevelt separated the emergency measures of the New Deal from 'normal' government activities such as making sure the budget was balanced. It was only when the crisis persisted and the 'emergency' measures themselves became 'normal' that Roosevelt changed his philosophy of the role of government. The New Deal did send American government in new directions; but there is a powerful argument that initially at least it was driven there more by necessity than from a coherent blueprint for change.

Other questions ask you about the success of the New Deal.

**5.** Was the New Deal a political and social success but an economic failure?
**6.** What was achieved by the New Deal?

These questions ask you to evaluate the New Deal. It is probably a good idea to separate out its political, social and economic impacts and to write a section on each. Alternatively, in your planning, you could draw up a chart with three columns:

|  | Effects of the New Deal |  |
|---|---|---|
| Political |  |  |
| Social |  |  |
| Economic |  |  |

Then you could expand upon these in your notes. However, it is important to make sure you evaluate how successful the measures you have considered were. You also need to explain why they were successful or unsuccessful. Clearly, politically the New Deal saw the federal government involved in more aspects of the country than ever before. The role of government was greatly enhanced. However, Roosevelt was still dependent on the support of conservatives within the Democratic Party. When he went too far, as with the case of the Supreme Court, he was defeated. Moreover, as events were to show in the later 1930s, he was still limited in his actions by what Congress would support. Socially the electorate began to look upon the federal government as their benefactor. However, the New Deal was divisive with the rich, in particular, opposing its policies. The government had tried to effect economic recovery but had largely failed. The return to recession in 1937 demonstrated that the economy had become dependent on government injections. If Roosevelt learned this lesson it was largely an unwelcome and unintended one.

Some questions ask you who benefited from the New Deal. Typical examples are:

**7.** Which groups in American society benefited from the New Deal and in what ways?
**8.** Which groups in society supported and which groups opposed the New Deal?

In answering these questions it is important to avoid two things: i) writing lists, and ii) oversimplification.

You may like to begin your planning by making a three column chart.

| Events | Supporters | Opponents of the New Deal |
|--------|-----------|---------------------------|
|        |           |                           |

You could then list the groups which supported the New Deal and those which opposed it. Note that the same groups might support or oppose it at different times. Why was this? You will need to account for changes in attitudes. It would be helpful to begin with a consideration of what the New Deal was designed to do, i.e. to put an end to the Depression. However, as time went on, it became apparent that this would involve massive government intervention through relief schemes that benefited the unemployed and did effect a partial recovery. But as more schemes were developed costing more money, Roosevelt's tax policies alienated many of the wealthy classes. His expansion of government intervention upset conservatives. The limitations of his schemes angered radicals. However, he did retain the affection of the majority of the electorate largely through his personal charisma. The poorer elements had great faith in him, although how far the New Deal actually addressed their needs is debatable. At best it was a start.

## Source-based questions on Chapter 7

### 1. A Letter to Roosevelt

Study carefully the letter to Roosevelt on pages 121–2. Answer the following questions.

**a)** Why do you think the writer wrote this letter? *(5 marks)*
**b)** What does the letter tell you about the attitude of ordinary people towards Roosevelt? *(5 marks)*

## 2. WPA

Study carefully the lyrics of the song 'Leaning on a Shovel' on page 126. Answer the following questions.

**a)** Explain the meaning of the following references: i) TVA (line 2) (2 marks), ii) Karl Marx (line 9) (2 marks), iii) the Dies Committee (line 10). (2 marks)
**b)** What is the message in these lyrics? *(4 marks)*
**c)** Using your own knowledge, assess how accurately this song reflects what actually happened. *(12 marks)*

## 3. The 1936 Presidential Election

Study carefully the cartoon on page 134. Answer the following questions.

**a)** What is the message in this cartoon? *(5 marks)*
**b)** Is the message of this cartoon supportive of Roosevelt? Explain your answer carefully. *(5 marks)*

## 4. The New Republic's Evaluation of Roosevelt's Second Term of Office

Study carefully the extract from the New Republic on pages 145. Answer the following questions.

**a)** Study the following statement: 'Since the expenditure of relief – even the insufficient amounts recently appropriated – has been the principal target of the administration's enemies, this accomplishment alone would be sufficient reason for support of the New Deal' (lines 7–10).
　**i)** Explain the statement in your own words. *(3 marks)*
　**ii)** Is this statement biased? Explain your answer carefully. *(4 marks)*
**b)** The authors say 'These years have seen no return to the conditions of 1932 or 1933, to be sure' (lines 19–20). Is this statement true? Explain your answer carefully with reference to your own knowledge. *(5 marks)*
**c)** According to lines 24–8, how are the President and business spokesman at variance over the means by which they would effect economic recovery? *(4 marks)*
**d) (i)** List the successes and failures of Roosevelt's second administration as given in this extract. *(4 marks)*
　**(ii)** What is its overall judgement on Roosevelt's second administration? Explain your answer with careful reference to the source. *(10 marks)*

# 8 The New Deal: an Evaluation

## POINTS TO CONSIDER

On first reading this chapter, consider on what bases we can evaluate the New Deal. In this chapter four are suggested: relief, recovery and reform, the criteria offered by Roosevelt himself in an early fireside chat; its impact on afro-caribbeans and women; how historians have assessed the New Deal; and how different the USA was at the end of it from what it had been like in 1919. How far had the New Deal changed the USA?

## 1 Introduction

> **KEY ISSUE**  Statistics of the New Deal can be viewed in different ways.

According to Ed Johnson, the Democratic Governor of Colorado, the New Deal was 'the worst fraud ever perpetrated on the American people'. While this view may be extreme, it can be argued that on the surface at least, the actual achievements of the New Deal do seem rather slender. In 1933, 18 million Americans were unemployed and in 1939, 9 million were still out of work. The national total of personal income stood at $86 billion in 1929 and only $73 billion in 1939, despite a population increase of 9 million during the course of the decade. The government seemed reconciled to a permanent unemployment figure of at least 5 million. One in five Americans required some sort of relief in 1939. In terms of prices, if one took the 1926 index as 100, in 1929 it stood at 95.3, in 1933 at 65.9, in 1937 at 86.3 and in 1939 at 77.1. Wages averaged $25.03 per week in 1929 and $23.86 ten years later. The Federal Reserve Board charted the physical volume of industrial production; taking 100 as an average in the years 1935-9, in 1929 the index stood at 110; in 1932, 58; in 1937, 113; in 1938, in the wake of the 'Roosevelt recession', 88; and in 1939, 109. On the surface, these figures are not impressive. However, the significance of statistics can often be assessed differently. One could argue, for example, that the New Deal decreased unemployment by 50 per cent; the New Deal saw farm incomes rise by the same amount; and that four out of five Americans did not require relief by 1939. Furthermore, because prices fell more than wages, people in work could afford to buy more as a result of the New Deal. Clearly any evaluation of the New Deal needs to go beyond statistics. Nor should one forget the enormity of the problems facing Roosevelt in 1933. No incoming President faced greater economic difficulties; and these were compounded by a desperate loss of confidence among both producers and consumers.

## 2 Relief, Recovery and Reform

> **KEY ISSUE** How may the New Deal be assessed in terms of relief,
> recovery and reform?

These aims offer a convenient compartmentalisation of the New Deal.
However, they are not meant to be seen as strictly separate. Some
measures could encompass two or more of them. The WPA, for
example, offered both relief to the unemployed and a boost to economic recovery through public works schemes. No measure was
initiated to fit into any one criterion. New Deal legislation, it should
be remembered, came about largely in response to crises with little
thought about the niceties of where in any blueprint it might fit.
However, as these goals of relief, recovery and reform were mentioned collectively as being the aims of the New Deal, it seems appropriate to use them for purposes of evaluation.

### a) Relief

One of the greatest achievements of the New Deal was in changing
the expectations of the role of federal government. This was particularly true of help for the less fortunate members of society. Relief
agencies such as FERA and the WPA were set up to offer hope to millions. There were new departures in governmental responsibilities.
The Social Security Act was not strictly a relief measure as it was
financed through contributions paid by recipients. But it did set up a
national system of old age pensions and unemployment benefit for
the first time. While it is true that the amounts spent were inadequate
for the needs of a population suffering from a prolonged depression,
important precedents were set by this legislation. It could be built on
in the future. Never before had the federal government become
involved in direct relief or benefits. Roosevelt initially saw relief agencies as only temporary expedients until economic recovery was
achieved; but in offering direct relief he significantly enhanced the
role of federal government. In addition, this led to a greater role for
state and local governments as partners – however unwillingly at first
– in many of the programmes. The growth in expenditure on welfare
tells its own story. In 1930 states spent $9 million; by 1940 this figure
had risen to $479 million. A further $480 million was spent on unemployment benefit. Before this they had spent nothing. Millions of
people began to see the federal government as their saviour. It was
through social reform that it first directly spoke to them. It was
through the provision of relief and benefits that many people first
became aware of a president not as a distant figure who meant little
to the likes of them but as someone who was interested in them and
who cared about them. It was partly due to the Depression that had

destroyed much of what people had previously believed in, and partly through the programmes of the New Deal which helped them, that more people took part in presidential elections in the 1930s. In 1920 and 1924 only 49 per cent of the electorate bothered to vote in the presidential elections; in 1928 and 1932 the figure rose to 57 per cent, and by 1936 and 1941 it was 62 per cent. Because of the provision of relief and benefits, more and more people felt they had a stake in their country. It made them feel they belonged.

## b) Recovery

The New Deal was less successful in effecting recovery. This was partly because many of the New Deal measures were contradictory. Roosevelt was a fiscal conservative wedded to the idea of the balanced budget and so he was reluctant to spend excessively on federal projects. He failed to see that massive government expenditure may be necessary to offset the reduction in spending in the private sector as a result of the Depression. Budget deficit fell from a high of $4.4 billion in 1936 to $2.7 billion in 1937 and $1.2 billion in 1938. Both of these figures were lower than the $2.8 billion deficit Hoover had run up in 1932 and over which Roosevelt had criticised him in the 1932 presidential election. Roosevelt was mistrustful of the efficacy of public works programmes. Keynes came out of a meeting with him in 1934 very disappointed, saying he doubted the President had really understood what he was saying. When Roosevelt did renege on earlier policy in the wake of the 1937 recession and offer $3.8 billion for public spending, it was not enough to make much of a difference.

The New Deal was designed to save the capitalist system in the USA. Roosevelt hoped his measures would facilitate a resurgence of capitalist confidence and expansion. We have already seen how many of his measures favoured big business. For example, the NRA codes were largely drawn up by their representatives. In the later years of the New Deal, Roosevelt was annoyed with big business because of its ingratitude for all the New Deal had done for it. However, he never doubted that the answer to economic problems lay largely in its hands. Again, it was his faith in capitalism and the market structure which led him to maintain fiscal conservatism and not adopt a plan of permanent massive state spending. It is interesting to note that the countries which did so, notably Sweden and Germany – albeit in the case of the latter on military expansion – overcame the Depression first. In contrast, by 1939, the USA was the slowest of the major countries to recover from depression.

## c) Reform

The New Deal was, when viewed in its totality, a programme of reform:

## i) Economic Reforms

Economic reforms were mainly intended to rescue the capitalist system from its worst excesses and to provide a more rational framework in which it could operate. For example, the banking system was reformed and made more efficient, particularly through the centralisation of banking in 1935. The iniquities of Wall Street and the holding companies were exposed and reformed. Roosevelt allowed trade unions to take their place in labour relations and reluctantly recognised that federal government had a role as an arbiter. In this sense the triangular partnership in labour relations between employers, employees and government was created.

## ii) Political Reforms

However reluctantly, Roosevelt came to realise that the expansion of government he had effected was to be permanent. He set up the Executive Office of the President to facilitate this expansion and ensure that the federal bureaucracy could cope with the demands being made upon it both then and in the future. His attempted reform of the Supreme Court failed but the Court nevertheless became more sympathetic to New Deal legislation, recognising the political realities of the later 1930s. The New Deal also saw a mirroring expansion in the functions of state and local government. The system again became more modern and able to address the needs of citizens in the twentieth century.

## iii) Social Reforms

Most importantly here was the expectation that the government would take responsibility for people's problems. The Social Security Act and the relief and job creation agencies expanded the role of government considerably.

However, having said this, it is important to reiterate that the New Deal should not be judged by targets it did not set out to achieve. It did not set out to change the capitalist structure. Those commentators who berate it as a lost opportunity to usher in a socialist economic system with greater equality of wealth and fully centralised planning are disappointed because they wanted the New Deal to be about these things. Unfortunately for them, it was not.

## 3 Other Evaluations of the New Deal

> **KEY ISSUE** How have people involved viewed the New Deal?

There follow five expert evaluations of the New Deal as a whole; all the commentators were interviewed by Studs Terkel in the late 1960s.[1]

## i) Gardiner C. Means

Gardiner C. Means was a New Deal staffer.

1  At the beginning of the New Deal, they called it a revolution. Then they began to say it wasn't a revolution. Our institutions were being shored up and maintained. What really happened was a revolution in point of view. We backed into the Twentieth Century describing our actual
5  economy in terms of the small enterprises of the Nineteenth Century. We were an economy of huge corporations, with a high degree of centralised control ... What Roosevelt and the New Deal did was to turn about and face the realities. It was this which produced the yeastiness of experimentation that made the New Deal what it was. A hundred
10  years from now, when historians look back on it, they will say a big corner was turned. People agreed that the old things didn't work. What ran through the whole New Deal was finding a way to make things work. Before that, Hoover would loan money to farmers to keep their mules alive but wouldn't loan money to keep children alive. This was
15  perfectly right within the framework of classical thinking. If an individual couldn't get enough to eat, it was because he wasn't on the ball. It was his responsibility. The New Deal said: Anybody who is unemployed isn't necessarily unemployed because he's shiftless.

## ii) Raymond Moley

Raymond Moley was a member of the original 'Brains' Trust'. However, he disagreed with the way the New Deal was going after 1935.

1  The first New Deal was a radical departure from American life. It put more power in the central government. At the time, it was necessary, especially in the farm area of our economy. Left to itself, farming was in a state of anarchy. Beyond that there was no need to
5  reorganise in industry. We merely needed to get the farms prospering again and create a market for the industrial products in the cities. The second New Deal was an entirely different thing. My disenchantment began then. Roosevelt didn't follow any particular policy after 1936. Our economy began to slide downhill – our unem-
10  ployment increased – after that, until 1940. This is something liberals are not willing to recognise. It was the war that saved the economy and saved Roosevelt ... I think if it weren't for the war, Roosevelt would probably have been defeated in 1940. You would probably have had a more business-minded Administration: less cen-
15  tralising on the part of Washington. More normal conditions would have prevailed.

## iii) David Kennedy

David Kennedy was a member of the Federal Reserve Board.

1 We really had not made a substantial recovery from the deep
Depression of the early Thirties. Unemployment was still very high. The
New Deal programs were not stimulating the way people thought.
There was a sort of defeatist attitude – that the Government just had
5 to do all this for the people. It was not until the war, with its economic
thrust, that we pulled out of it. The war got us out of it, not the New
Deal policies ... Roosevelt, with his silver tongue brought words of
hope. He started many things going but they were turned on and off.
We had the NRA, the WPA and these things – they'd come and go.
10 You never could get clear cut decisions. One day one thing; the next
day, another. It was bedlam and confusion in Washington ... I felt we
were relying on the Government to save us. There was not enough
involvement in the private area to carry its share of the burden. I felt
people were losing the initiative to get out on their own instead of:
15 Please hand it to me.

## iv) Alfred Landon

Alfred Landon was Roosevelt's Republican opponent in the 1936
presidential election.

1 I was accused of being too much of a me-too New Dealer by some of
the staunch Republicans. They couldn't see the necessity of staying in
tune with the times. They were out of touch ... If you take Mr
Roosevelt's program today in light of what both Republican and
5 Democrats are standing for, he'd be pretty conservative.

## v) Christopher Lasch

Christopher Lasch, an historian of the American left, attempted an
historical analysis of the New Deal.

1 In retrospect, I don't think there was a revolutionary situation in
America in the early Thirties, certainly not the kind of situation that
would have led to socialism if the New Deal reforms hadn't been
carried out. There was a demand for vigorous, authoritative leadership.
5 Industrialists clamoured for central control, even nationalisation of
some industries. Harold Ickes, in his diary, talks of industrialists
descending on Washington, demanding that the Government take over
the oil industry. I think if a semblance of vigorous leadership hadn't been
forthcoming on the part of Roosevelt, there might have been built up
10 the kind of pressure that swept Mussolini into power in Italy. It is con-
ceivable, in other words, that the government might have been forced
into extreme measures, but I doubt these would have taken a left-wing
direction. The NRA was a clear example of how the New Deal worked.
All points of view were entertained. All kinds of advisers were sum-
15 moned up. People got together and at one point were simply put into
a room. Roosevelt said: You have to come up with something, whatever
it is. The result was a compromise between things labor wanted and

things business wanted ... But there were no clear lines of policy followed. The whole New Deal, as far as I can see, was really chaotic. All
20 kinds of experiments were being tried constantly. The immediate aim of
all the reforms was simply to end the Depression by whatever means
came to hand. It's a case study of what can happen if you don't have a
clear policy. That it (American society) would stay capitalist there was
no doubt. Other alternatives were excluded from the beginning, as a
25 range of serious ideas that might be considered. But within these shared
assumptions, two distinct points of view could be discerned. On the
one hand there were the so-called enlightened businessmen who
reflected the view of large, progressively minded corporations, who
recognised the need for regulation, the need to admit labor as a part-
30 ner in the industrial enterprise – as a junior and distinctly inferior, partner. They proposed to recognise labor's right to bargain and to enact
welfare programs, if for no other reason that to head off more drastic
proposals. On the other hand, there were the people who clung to a
laissez faire ideology, who resented all these measures, partly because
35 – the NRA being a beautiful example – they were clearly detrimental to
the interests of small, independent outfits. They were clearly in the
interests of giant corporations ...

# 4 Race and Gender

> **KEY ISSUE** What did the New Deal do for afro-caribbeans and
> women?

We have already seen that the New Deal did more for Native
Americans than past administrations, but critics have argued that it
did little for afro-caribbeans and women.

## a) Afro-caribbeans

Roosevelt needed the vote of Southern Democrats. A realist, he said,
'I did not choose the tools with which I must work'. Certainly, early in
the New Deal, Southern politicians were often his most loyal supporters. Not surprisingly therefore, the New Deal saw no civil rights legislation and many of its measures – the AAA for instance – worked
against afro-caribbeans. Afro-caribbeans suffered particularly badly in
the Depression, often being the last to be taken on and the first to be
fired. Many poorly paid, menial jobs previously reserved for them
were now taken by whites. NRA codes allowed for afro-caribbeans to
be paid less than whites for doing the same jobs. Some afro-
caribbeans called the NRA the 'Negro-run-around' because it was so
unfair to them. The CCC was run by a southern racist who did little
to encourage afro-caribbeans to join: those who did faced strict seg-
regation. Anti-lynching bills were introduced into Congress in 1934

and 1937, but Roosevelt did nothing to support either and both were eventually defeated.

Despite these negative points, one of the most important political features of the New Deal years was the realignment of afro-caribbeans in the North who were able to vote (less than 5 per cent of afro-caribbeans in the South could vote). Traditionally afro-caribbeans voted Republican because this was the party which had fought the Civil War in part to end slavery. In 1932, of 15 afro-caribbean wards in nine major cities, Roosevelt won only four; in 1936, he won nine, and by 1940, all 15. In some afro-caribbean areas of cities, notably Harlem in New York, Roosevelt won 85 per cent of the vote. A Gallop Poll in 1936 showed that nationally 76 per cent of afro-caribbeans intended to vote for Roosevelt. Many afro-caribbeans saw him as as much a saviour as poor whites did. His portrait hung in many afro-caribbean homes. In 1936 there were 30 afro-caribbean delegates to the Democratic Convention and much to the disgust of Southerners the first afro-caribbean Congressman, Arthur Mitchell, delivered the opening speech. We need to look beyond the surface of the New Deal to explain this significant shift of allegiance.

Many New Deal administrators, notably Harry Hopkins and Harold Ickes, showed concern for afro-caribbeans and tried to make sure they were included in relief programmes. Eleanor Roosevelt was determined to do all she could to stop racism. She was able to ensure prominent afro-caribbeans met with the President to explain the problems faced by their race and she herself made a public statement in 1938 when she sat in the 'coloured' section at the Conference of Human Welfare in Birmingham, Alabama. When the afro-caribbean singer Marion Anderson was refused permission to sing before an integrated audience at Constitution Hall in Washington in 1939, Harold Ickes arranged for her to give a concert in front of 75,000 people, including Mrs Roosevelt, at the Lincoln Memorial. These gestures were significant in giving official respectability to the notion that racism was wrong and helped afro-caribbean leaders gain confidence in their own struggles. When A. Phillip Randolph, head of the afro-caribbean trade union, Brotherhood of Sleeping Car Porters, threatened a march on Washington in 1940 to protest against racism in defence factories, Roosevelt set up a Fair Employment Practices Committee to stop such behaviour.

Moreover, the President did employ more afro-caribbeans in government, notably, as we saw on page 125, Mary McLeod Bethune at the NYA. However, while there were more afro-caribbeans in government office, it seems an exaggeration to speak as some did of a 'afro-caribbean' cabinet' addressing race issues. The Civil Service tripled the number of afro-caribbeans in its employment between 1932 and 1941 to 150,000. There was also some positive discrimination, notably again in the NYA where afro-caribbean officials were usually appointed in areas where afro-caribbeans predominated.

It will be seen, then, that if there were few official measures specifically to benefit afro-caribbeans, there were important symbolic gestures. There were more afro-caribbeans with the ear if not of the President then of important figures close to him, and millions of afro-caribbeans benefited from relief measures which, if still favouring whites, gave them more help than they had ever previously received.

## b) Women

Women held more important posts in government during the New Deal era than at any time before or after until the 1990s. Mrs Roosevelt was one of the most politically active first ladies; as Secretary of Labor, Frances Perkins was only one of many women holding government office; and Ruth Bryan Owen became the first female ambassador (to Denmark). Many prominent women had come together through expertise in social work, which was, of course, an asset for designing many New Deal measures. Unfortunately, when government priorities changed with the onset of war, much of their influence was lost.

The New Deal, in fact, did little for women. Unlike afro-caribbeans, they did not tend to vote in a bloc and so they were not particularly wooed by politicians. Much New Deal legislation worked against them. In 1933, for example, the Economy Act forbade members of the same family from working for federal government and so many wives lost their jobs. 75 per cent of those losing their jobs through this measure were women. We have seen on page 70 that many measures to curb the Depression took jobs away particularly from married women. The New Deal did nothing to reverse this process. NRA codes allowed for unequal wages and some agencies such as the CCC barred women entirely. Women suffered particularly in the professions where, even by 1940, about 90 per cent of jobs were still filled by men. There was a strong emphasis that in the job market, helping the man was the priority and where women did find employment – which many had to do to balance the family budget – it tended often to be in low-status, poorly paid jobs. On average during the 1930s, at $525 per annum, women earned half the average wage of men.

## 5 Legacy of the New Deal

> **KEY ISSUE** What were the long-term effects of the New Deal?

The legacy of the New Deal was profound. While it may not have effected a social, political or economic revolution, many attitudes in the USA were fundamentally altered as a result of it.

## a) Political Realignments

The New Deal created the coalition of afro-caribbeans, urban blue-collar workers, unions, Southern conservatives and eastern liberals that survived largely intact in the Democratic Party until Ronald Reagan began to eat away at the blue-collar vote in the 1980s. The Democratic Party became recognised as the party of social reform; its agenda was the one that contained the programmes to help the have-nots in society. Unfairly or otherwise, the Republicans came increasingly to be seen as the Party of wealth and big business, the Party which did little for the common man. These attitudes survived largely until the 1980s.

## b) Changes in the Political System

The New Deal saw the growth of the executive vis à vis other branches of government. Increasingly, legislation was initiated by the executive, and state governments were involved in joint programmes which not only increased their own activities but also made them more dependent on federal government for funding and action. Americans began to look to federal government rather than the states for action to meet problems. In addition, the Supreme Court began to adopt a more flexible view of the constitution. The idea of the division of powers, formulated in the constitution, began to break down in order to give the executive more freedom to address what were perceived to be the needs of the country. This was possibly inevitable and may even have happened without the Depression. President Harding had certainly seen the need to expand the role of federal government and Hoover had believed the government should take a major role for good in the life of the nation. This development was not just a facet of federal government. State and local expenditure had increased from $1 billion in 1902 to $10 billion by 1938. Quite simply, no country could progress successfully in the twentieth century with a nineteenth-century governmental system. In this sense, the Depression and New Deal accentuated a process already underway. However, there is an alternative argument that together they may even have stifled it. Some historians, notably Arthur Schlesinger, Jr., have argued that reforms in American government usually take place in times of prosperity. They point to the relative prosperity of the Progressive Era in the first decades of the twentieth century as an example. On the basis of this, there would have been pressure for reform in the 1930s if the prosperity had continued. In this sense the Depression may have acted as a break on reform. The New Deal, which was in effect an operation to preserve the existing structure, may have been substituted by something far more radical.

## c) Support for the Existing Political Structure

Perhaps the most important legacy of the New Deal was that it restored hope and confidence in the capitalist and democratic systems of the USA. This was in a large amount due to the personal charisma of Roosevelt himself and the trust people were prepared to bestow on him. However, we have seen that there was comparatively little support for extremist parties even during the height of the Depression. The vast majority of Americans wanted the existing system to provide the solutions to the Depression. Some historians have argued that the New Deal averted revolution in the USA. This is one of the fascinating 'what if?' questions in history. We shall never know, had Roosevelt not been there in 1932, what measures a different President would have attempted nor how frustrated Americans may have become. We have seen that the ideas behind many of the New Deal measures pre-dated Roosevelt's presidency and that others were initiated in Congress. One historian wrote that Roosevelt 'took his place at the head of the procession only when it was clear where the procession was going'. Whether this was true or not, there can be little doubt that the New Deal was designed to preserve the established structure. Some historians have argued that it was effectively a holding operation until recovery was effected by the onset of war. Again, we can say with hindsight that this is undoubtedly true. Unfortunately, people at the time do not possess hindsight. It would be absurd to suggest that Roosevelt consciously adopted the New Deal as a holding operation until war came. No one could accurately foresee war until comparatively late in the 1930s. Even then there was a considerable body of opinion that felt the USA should have nothing to do with the conflict, including refusing to sell the belligerents any weapons. When evaluated the New Deal needs to stand on its own merits. In this context we have seen that it had seemed to have lost direction by 1939, and that Roosevelt's administration was increasingly neutralised by a hostile Congress. Had Roosevelt not decided to stand again in 1940, and had not foreign affairs begun to dominate, it is difficult to foresee what would have happened in the USA. In an election dominated by foreign issues, the Republican candidate Wendell Wilkie did oppose the growing power of the state. However, by this time economic recovery was on its way due to the European war and economic issues did not feature heavily in the campaigns. So we are left with another 'what if?' question that is basically unanswerable.

The New Deal came to the salvation of capitalism and in so doing enhanced the power of the state in a way unprecedented in American history. It did not do enough to address the severity of the problems facing the USA but there is no doubt that it broke away from existing norms particularly through direct relief and institutional reform. It set important precedents for the future. Perhaps the final verdict may go to the editors of the Economist magazine: 'Mr Roosevelt may have given the wrong answers to many of his problems. But he is at least the first President of modern America who has asked the right questions'.

# 6 Historiography of the New Deal

**KEY ISSUE**  How have historians regarded the New Deal?

In the years following the New Deal, historians were generally supportive. Some argued that the enhanced role of the government in responsibility for people's welfare marked the growing maturity of the nation – effecting what Carl Degler called, 'a third American Revolution.'[2] Leuchtenburg wrote that 'it is hard to think of another period in the whole history of the republic that was so fruitful or a crisis that was met with such imagination'.[3] In the 1960s however, historians of 'The New Left' such as H. Zinn and Paul Conkin became more critical. They tended to see the New Deal as a wasted opportunity for radical change. It was felt that the piecemeal solutions of the New Deal enabled capitalism to prevail. In the words of Paul Conkin, 'the story of the New Deal is a sad story, the ever recurring story of what might have been.'[4] However as we have seen in this chapter, the New Deal was not intended to effect radical change, and historians have tended to criticise it for something it was not rather than to criticise it on its own merits. In the 1970s, historians and economists notably Milton Friedman often attacked the New Deal for the opposite reasons: that it had set the USA on the wrong course. Government spending, they argued, fuelled inflation; Governments taking responsibility for people's livelihood fostered welfare dependency and stifled entrepreneurial creativity. These historians favoured the working of the free market; they saw the election of President Reagan in 1980 as a turning-point, reversing the movement begun by the New Deal for governments to take responsibility for people's lives.[5]

More recent studies have focussed on two elements:

a) the strength of conservative opposition and the readiness of the American people to accept traditional remedies. The conclusion is that there was no appetite for radical change. People wanted capitalism to work;

b) the impact of the New Deal on specific groups and regions, a kind of 'bottom-up' history which enables us to examine the impact of the New Deal on the ground.[6]

# 7 Conclusion

> **KEY ISSUE** What conclusions can be drawn about the impact of
> the New Deal?

We saw in Chapter 1 that the first decades of the twentieth century
had seen an unprecedented growth in government. Of the three
Republican Presidents of the 1920s, only Coolidge sought to redress
this. Therefore, the New Deal continued a process already underway,
although into avenues that would have horrified earlier Presidents.
There is a story that former President Hoover refused to apply for a
social security card. Although he objected to being 'numberfied', the
agency sent him one anyway as they did to everyone. The idea that
everyone in the country could be affected by any one federal government domestic measure would have been unthinkable in 1920.

Industrial relations had moved into the modern era with more of
a partnership between government, employers and unions. The government also recognised the importance of big business. While small
self-reliant businessmen may have been heroes in the American
dream, as we have seen, American capitalism grew in reality through
the power of big business. Although it may not always have been
realised at the time, it was largely the interests of big business that the
economic measures of the New Deal succeeded. The benefits of this
were clear during the war, when business infrastructure was relatively
easily able to adapt to large-scale armaments production.

Both people and states increasingly looked to the government for
help with their problems. The USA was beginning to become
urbanised to a more noticeable degree, and legislation such as the
1937 National Housing Act recognised this. The tensions we examined in Chapter 2 which resulted particularly from the rural-urban
divide had not gone away and have continued to resurface in
American history. Many of Roosevelt's supporters in the South later
turned against him because they felt legislation was increasingly
favouring northern cities to the detriment of rural areas. However,
even in the countryside things had changed. Agencies such as the
TVA and REA had helped rural areas move into a modern era with
their provision of facilities such as electrical power. Farmers, the self-
reliant heroes of American mythology, were now expecting loans and
subsidies from the government through the AAA. The tentacles of
government, it seemed, were everywhere. The USA had moved from
a land of self-reliant individualism with very little government interference to one where the government increasingly took responsibility
for people's lives and welfare. The Depression had showed that the
economy was not self-righting and that the American Dream was
largely impossible to realise unaided, however much initiative and
ability to work hard one might possess. In the end, the Depression

had eroded much of the American mythology we considered in Chapter 1, particularly the notion of self-reliance. It became necessary in the 1930s to address a harsh reality and the significance of the New Deal was that this is what it did.

## References

1   S. Turkel, *Hard Times* (Penguin, 1970).
2   R. Biles, *A New Deal for the American People* (North Illinois University Press, 1991), p. 2.
3   W. Leuchtenburg, *The Achievement of the New Deal*, in (ed) H. Sitkoff, *Fifty Years Later: the New Deal Evaluated* (Alfred A. Knopf, 1985) p. 213.
4   In R. Biles, *op. cit.*, p. 3.
5   A.J. Badger, *The New Deal* (Macmillan, 1989), p. 4.
6   R. Biles, *op. cit.*, p. 3.

**Summary diagram**
The New Deal: An Evaluation

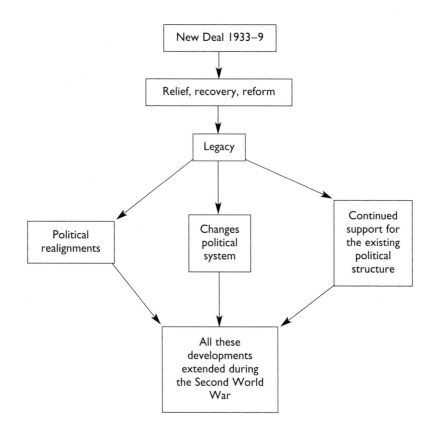

## Working on Chapter 8

When making notes on this chapter, you should: **i)** consider how effective the New Deal was in terms of its own criteria of relief, recovery and reform; **ii)** examine what it did in terms of race and gender; **iii)** consider its legacy and how historians have regarded it over time; and **iv)** examine how much the USA had changed between 1919 and 1941. You should then be able to make your own evaluation of the New Deal. What do you think it achieved? Could it and should it have done more?

## Source-based and structured questions on Chapter 8

Read section 3, pages 154–7, which contains all the sources. Answer the following questions.

### 1. Gardiner C. Means

**a)** Explain carefully what is meant by the statement, 'We backed into the Twentieth Century describing our economy in terms of the small enterprises of the Nineteenth Century'. (page 155, lines 4–5) *(5 marks)*

**b)** How does this contrast with the realities? (line 8) *(3 marks)*

**c)** Explain the phrase, 'Before that Hoover would loan money to farmers to keep their mules alive but wouldn't loan money to keep children alive'. (lines 13–14) *(5 marks)*

**d)** What does this writer see as the main changes made by the New Deal? *(7 marks)*

### 2. Raymond Moley

**a)** What does he see as important about the First New Deal? *(5 marks)*

**b)** Why did he oppose the Second New Deal? *(5 marks)*

### 3. David Kennedy

**a)** On what points concerning economic recovery does Kennedy agree with Raymond Moley? *(5 marks)*

**b)** Does Kennedy support or oppose the New Deal? Give reasons for your answer. *(7 marks)*

### 4. Alfred Landon

**a)** Although he was Roosevelt's opponent in the 1936 presidential election, Landon nevertheless says that he supported the New Deal. Why do you think this was? *(5 marks)*

### 5. Christopher Lasch

**a)** Is this extract for or against the New Deal? Explain your answer carefully. *(5 marks)*

**b)** What did Lasch see as the threat to American democracy? *(5 marks)*

**c)** Expain how, according to the author, the NRA could be used to describe how the New Deal worked. *(5 marks)*

**d)** On what points might Lasch agree with Kennedy? Explain your answer carefully. *(5 marks)*

**e)** On what issue might Lasch agree with Means? Explain your answer carefully. *(5 marks)*

## 6. *Study all the sources again*

**a)** All give different judgments about the New Deal.

**i)** Draw up a chart listing each author and the judgements he makes about the New Deal. Use the headings set out below:

| Author | Comments |
|--------|----------|
|        |          |

**ii)** How many comments are essentially the same? List the authors who appear to agree with each other.

**iii)** How many comments are essentially different from all the others? List the authors who appear to disagree with each other.

**iv)** Account for the similarities and differences in these evaluations. *(15 marks)*

**b)** How adequate are these evaluations in enabling you to make an informed judgement on the New Deal? Explain your answer carefully. *(10 marks)*

**c)** Using all these sources and your own knowledge, explain why the New Deal has continued to be an area of debate among historians. *(15 marks)*

This last question is a mini-essay. You need to use the sources to show how opinions differed among those actually involved in the New Deal. You need then to go on to look at historical interpretations. Historians often embrace the values of their own age. The 1960s were a time of radical thought, when many wanted wide-ranging changes in society, with the government taking far more responsibility for people's welfare. It is not surprising, then, that many historians thought the New Deal didn't go far enough in changing society. The 1970s and 1980s saw a reaction to what many felt to be too much government involvement in people's lives – therefore many historians were critical of the New Deal, which they saw as the precursor of this development. The later studies of specific groups and areas reflect the modern trend for 'bottom-up' history, to examine issues as they actually affected different groups of people differently in different regions of the USA. Always bear in mind, though, that an impartial historian should evaluate an issue in terms of what it set out to do at the time – not what we may have preferred it to have set out to do from the perspective of our own modern day values. We have to examine what people thought at the time.

# Further Reading

The following are readable and stimulating books that cover the entire period dealt with in this book.

**Peter Fearon**, *War, Prosperity and Depression*, Philip Allan, 1987

**David Kennedy**, *Freedom From Fear*, Oxford History of the United States 1999

**Donald R. McCoy**, *Coming of Age*, Pelican History of the United States 6, Penguin, 1973

**Michael E. Parrish**, *Anxious Decades*, W. W. Norton, 1992

*War, Prosperity and Depression* is an economic history and will appeal primarily to those with an interest in and knowledge of economic issues. *Coming of Age* offers more of a political and economic history that emphasises the continuity of the period. *Anxious Decades* and *Freedom From Fear* are largely syntheses of modern American scholarship; both of them are very well written and rich in narrative detail.

You can also read with profit the relevant chapters in:

**Hugh Brogan**, *The Pelican History of the United States*, Penguin, 1986

**Tom Kemp**, *The Climax Of Capitalism*, Longman, 1990

**Paul Johnson**, *A History of the American People*, Weidenfeld and Nicolson, 1997

**Daniel Snowman**, *USA, The Twenties to Vietnam*, B.T. Batsford, 1968

Brogan gives a brilliant panorama of US history. Johnson's book is always stimulating and far less critical of the 1920s than many other works. *The Climax of Capitalism* offers a concise economic history written in lay terms with lots of useful statistical evidence. Snowman, although dated, gives very useful analytic insights.

One of the most influential historians of the Wall Street Crash and Depression is **J.K. Galbraith**. Useful introductions to his work can be found in two articles, 'Days of Boom and Bust' and 'The Wall Street Crash' in *Purnell; History of the Twentieth Century, Volume 3*. You should also read *The Great Crash 1929*, Penguin, 1975.

Specific texts on the 1930s and Roosevelt include;

**D.K. Adams**, *Franklin D Roosevelt and the The New Deal*, Historical Association, 1979

**Anthony J. Badger**, *The New Deal*, Macmillan, 1989

**Roger Biles**, A New Deal for the American People, North Illinois University Press, 1991

**Paul K. Conkin**, *The New Deal*, Routledge and Kegan Paul, 1967

**William Leuchtenburg**, *The FDR Years*, Columbia University Press, 1995

**Michael Simpson**, *Franklin D. Roosevelt*, Historical Association Studies, 1989

**T.H. Watkins**, *The Great Depression*, Little, Brown and Co., 1993

Adams is particularly useful on the philosophy of the New Deal. Both Badger and Biles give a useful synthesis of recent scholarship. Both books are particularly well written and insightful and are also particularly good on the historiography of the New Deal. Conkin gives a relatively short analysis of the New Deal that wanted it to have been more radical. *The FDR Years* is a collection of essays written over time by one of the experts on the period. Simpson has written a short, concise biography with the needs of students in mind. Watkins's work is lavishly illustrated, a book to accompany a major television documentary of the period; it is particularly good on factual detail.

**Sources**
Particularly useful as primary evidence and readily available are **Frederick Allen**'s two memoirs: *Only Yesterday*, Harper and Row, 1931, and *Since Yesterday*, Harper and Row, 1940. They have been reprinted many times. **Studs Terkel**, *Hard Times*, Penguin, 1970, is rich with oral evidence from the period. **John Major**, *The New Deal*, Longman, 1968, is a very useful collection of documents.

# Index